Sport in the Global Society

General Editor: J.A. Mangan

THE CHANGING FACE OF THE FOOTBALL BUSINESS

D0224181

SPORT IN THE GLOBAL SOCIETY

General Editor: J.A. Mangan

The interest in sports studies around the world is growing and will continue to do so. This unique series combines aspects of the expanding study of *sport in the global society*, providing comprehensiveness and comparison under one editorial umbrella. It is particularly timely, with studies in the cultural, economic, ethnographic, geographical, political, social, anthropological, sociological and aesthetic elements of sport proliferating in institutions of higher education.

Eric Hobsbawm once called sport one of the most significant practices of the late nineteenth century. Its significance was even more marked in the late twentieth century and will continue to grow in importance into the new millennium as the world develops into a 'global village' sharing the English language, technology and sport.

Other Titles in the Series

THE CHANGING FACE OF THE FOOTBALL BUSINESS

Supporters Direct

Editors

SEAN HAMIL, JONATHAN MICHIE, CHRISTINE OUGHTON and STEVEN WARBY

Birkbeck College, University of London

FRANK CASS
LONDON • PORTLAND, OR

First published in 2001 in Great Britain by
FRANK CASS PUBLISHERS
Newbury House, 900 Eastern Avenue
London, IG2 7HH

and in the United States of America by
FRANK CASS PUBLISHERS
c/o ISBS, 5824 N.E. Hassalo Street
Portland, Oregon 97213-3644

Website: www.frankcass.com

British Library Cataloguing in Publication Data

The changing face of the football business: supporters direct. –
(Sport in the global society; no. 26)
1. Soccer – Economic aspects – Great Britain 2. Soccer teams –
Great Britain – Management 3. Soccer fans
I. Hamil, Sean
338.4´7796334´0941

ISBN 0-7146-5136-2 (cloth)
ISBN 0-7146-8163-6 (paper)
ISSN 1368-9789

Library of Congress Cataloging-in-Publication Data

The changing face of the football business : supporters direct /
editors, Sean Hamil ... [et al.]..
    p. cm. — (Sport in the global society, ISSN 1368-9789)
Includes bibliographical references and index.
  ISBN 0-7146-5136-2 — ISBN 0-7146-8163-6
1. Soccer—Great Britain—Management. 2. Soccer fans—Great Britain.
3. Soccer—Economic aspects—Great Britain. I. Hamil, Sean. II. Cass
series—sport in the global society.
GV944.G7 C43 2000
796.334´0941—dc21   00-011683

This group of studies first appeared as a special issue of *Soccer and Society*
(ISSN 1466-0970), Vol.1, No.3, Autumn 2000, published by Frank Cass

Printed in Great Britain by Antony Rowe Ltd., Chippenham, Wilts

Contents

Foreword

There is no doubt the game has changed. With all-seater stadiums, huge franchising and sponsorship deals, and the explosion of satellite television revenues and the promise of pay-per-view, does the game still need the regular match-going fan to turn up week upon week to cheer on the team? There is no doubt in my mind – yes it does. Without the fans the game is nothing. What would be the point?

The television money is welcome but it's no substitute for the fans getting behind the team when you're a goal down with five minutes to go. And while Old Trafford is now a magnificent stadium, I had to make some well-reported complaints at the lack of atmosphere during some of last season's games. The fans responded magnificently for the next game, against Fiorentina, lifting the team to a great display and an impressive victory.

The true measure of fans' loyalty, though, is not the sell-out crowds during a period of success like we at Manchester United have enjoyed over the past decade. It's turning out during the bleak years, when your team is struggling, losing, possibly being relegated. That is what the long-serving Manchester United fans can point to – even when the team dropped to the old Second Division in the early 1970s, they had a higher average gate than did any of the top division teams. Success in football comes and goes. And with it no doubt some fair weather supporters. But the real fans stick with their teams through thick and thin. It's not just about winning – it's about loyalty. That must be respected. It must be repaid. Any football club that forgets that does so at its peril.

What would I know about hard times, some might ask, when I can go and buy the likes of Jaap Stam? It was not always like that, I can tell you. When I was managing St Mirren I knew I had to buy an experienced player if we were to make any sort of impact at all. The man I needed was Jackie Copland, a seasoned and tough centre-half. The transfer fee was £17,000. St Mirren had £3,000. Where was I to get the other £14,000? The Supporters' Association lent the money.

Those supporters knew that I was totally committed to the club, to them, and to building the strong bond that a successful team must have with the local community. My first appeal to the fans at St Mirren had not been to ask for money. It was to drive round the town in the van demanding – not asking, demanding – that the local residents get down to the ground to support their team. The crowd soon grew tenfold from the low level to which gates had sunk before my arrival. It was not because of me as an individual. It was about having a manager who cared passionately for his team and expected the local community to do likewise.

It has been the same story at every club I have been at – from St Mirren to Manchester United. A healthy club is based on strong links with the local community and a bond of loyalty with the fans. It is great of course to have players of the calibre of Jaap Stam wanting to play for United. And the fans appreciate the efforts he made to move to our club. But what they also love is to have true United fans such as the Neville brothers playing for their team. Local lads like Paul Scholes. At the time of writing there has been much speculation about how much Scholes might be sold to an Italian team for. I have no problem in valuing him. Priceless. You just can't buy commitment and loyalty like that – never mind the talent.

So for me the big money signings and the rest will never change the fact that the lifeblood of football is the fans. That is why I welcome the launch of Supporters Direct and am pleased to write the Foreword to this book. There is no doubt that there has been a change in the game. I am not talking about the massive increase in commercialism now. I am talking about the fans' reaction. The rise in supporter activism over the past few years, and in particular the response of fans to seeing their clubs floated on the Stock Exchange – the creation of supporter-shareholder groups who are demanding a say in their clubs. Quite right. Why should the future of their club lie solely in the hands of financial institutions in the City of London?

As the various authors of this book demonstrate, that voice can play a key role in cementing the bond between club, community and fans that is vital to football as a social, cultural and sporting institution. I cannot believe the way I am still quoted with my response to the amazing comeback at the Nou Camp – 'Football, eh? Bloody hell'. I see my friend Kevin Jaquiss has done it again in his essay. But the memory of the tens of thousands of United fans in and around the stadium that night makes me want to revise that quote – 'Football fans, eh? Bloody hell'. That passion, that commitment, that devotion. It cannot be bought and it certainly should not be cashed in. It needs to be rewarded, invested in, and nurtured through the next generation of supporters. For me that is what Supporters Direct is all about. That is why it is vital it succeeds. It must and I am sure it will.

ALEX FERGUSON
September 2000

Series Editor's Foreword

The Changing Face of the Football Business is a timely celebration of loyalty – in the words of Graham Greene in *The Heart of the Matter* – 'the sense that that is where we really belong'. Two soundbites from Sir Alex Ferguson's Foreword say it all: 'It [football] is not just about winning – it's about loyalty' which, he states rightly, is 'That passion, that commitment, that devotion [which] cannot be bought ...' Loyalty, of course, binds fan and club through thick and thin, bad times and good times, ''til death do us part'.

Soccer fat cats with fat wallets should now be held at bay. Enough is enough. Time for the fan to hold the high ground and Murdoch the low ground. This is what this sensible book shouts to the Heavens. And its case is strong.

As Adam Brown has said elsewhere:

> While all sections of the economy may have their own peculiarities, they share the fact that they are largely governed by the basic laws of supply and demand and competition between different suppliers of similar goods and services ... The crucial difference in understanding the dynamics of the football industry is that, for the vast majority who pay to go to games as well as for most of those who buy televised football, the motivation is an emotional support for a particular team. Thus consumption, and competition between firms for it, is different in football from almost any other major sporting industry or other areas of the entertainment business.[1]

And again he has stated more succinctly: 'Brand loyalty, rather than quality or value for money, is the determining factor in football 'consumption', an emotional commitment to the team which is above and beyond normal consumer choice',[2] with the result that fans, to paraphrase one recent observation, constitute a real asset of a truly intangible nature. It is an idiosyncratic but real investment, a commercial oddity, as Brown remarks, 'with too much cultural and social importance to be left [entirely] to market forces'.[3]

In *The Changing Face of the Football Business* the concern is effective supporter involvement in modern soccer and the creation of the means of ensuring that supporters have a responsible role in club life. As the contributors make abundantly clear, this can take many forms but the ultimate aim of them all is the democratization of football clubs so that once again soccer becomes the people's game.

The editors immediately strike the right note with their opening words in Chapter 1:

> Over the past decade there have been dramatic changes in the way football is organized as witnessed by the formation of the Premier League, the

introduction of all-seater stadiums, the increasing money from TV deals, the dramatic increase in the price of tickets, the transformation of clubs into Plcs, and growing media ownership of football clubs. Against this background of change one fact remains constant – football clubs need supporters if they are to survive and flourish ... Many examples ... will be found throughout this volume.' (p.1)

This support now requires formal mechanisms protected by law. Too often supporter loyalty has often brought poor returns; too often supporters have been the *last* consideration of football club directors. Time for change.

One of the great strengths of this important book is its practical approach to solving this scandal in the national game. Its commonsense aim is to make sure that soccer reaps 'the benefits of increased commercialization *while* [emphasis added] remaining the people's game' (p.9).

All power to the Editors' 'elbow'.

J.A. MANGAN
*International Research Centre
for Sport, Socialisation, Society,
University of Strathclyde*
September 2000

NOTES

1. Adam Brown, 'Taken to Task: The Football Task Force, Government and the Regulation of the People's Game', in Steve Greenfield and Guy Osborn (eds.), *Law and Sport in Contemporary Society* (London and Portland, OR: Frank Cass, 2000), p.256.
2. Ibid., p.259.
3. Ibid., p.263.

Preface and Acknowledgements

SEAN HAMIL, JONATHAN MICHIE,
CHRISTINE OUGHTON and STEVEN WARBY

This volume aims to follow up the key issue of supporter involvement in football clubs identified in our previous books, *A Game of Two Halves?*[1] and *Football in the Digital Age*.[2] Those books came from conferences organized by the Football Research Unit at Birkbeck College[3] and were collaborative efforts, featuring contributions from many leading policy-makers and analysts of the game. Likewise, the present volume came out of a January 2000 conference organized by the Football Research Unit on *Supporter Involvement in Football Clubs*. The issues raised at that conference are discussed in more detail in Chapter 1 below, but here we would like to acknowledge our gratitude to all those who attended and contributed to what was an extremely well-informed and constructive event. The chapters of this book are loosely based on the contributions made by the speakers at the January conference, and we are immensely grateful to all the authors for their contributions.

We hope this volume gives a thorough and comprehensive account of the growing movement behind football supporters seeking to play a responsible role in the life of their clubs. Supporter involvement in football clubs comes in many forms, from those supporters who belong to members' clubs or independent associations, to those who contribute to bulletin boards or fanzines, to those who seek more influence over how their club is actually run, and to those who already do play an active role in running their club. The Football Task Force took supporter involvement as one of its key areas of study, and came up with various recommendations in both its *Investing in the Community* and *Football: Commercial Issues* reports.[4] One of the key recommendations of the Task Force was support for establishing supporters' trusts, building on the positive experience at clubs such as Northampton Town FC.[5] Supporters' trusts enable supporters to come together as a group and represent their interests to the club, but unlike other fan associations, for the purposes of seeking direct representation. Trusts enable supporters to pool shares in their club to form a block shareholding. Such trusts can then be used to seek supporter representation at football clubs, ultimately at board level. The motivation of this initiative is nothing less than the democratization of football clubs. The Task Force succeeded in bringing together a broad coalition of those concerned for the future of the game, and there was a clear consensus that football needed change. Bringing supporters into their clubs, reversing the perception of them as turnstile fodder, and drawing on their support can only be to the longer-term benefit of the game.

How supporters can do this, and the experiences of those who have established such trusts, is one of the central themes of this book. We hope that the issues covered here, and the example of those who have already begun to take more of an active role in the running of their clubs, will inspire others to follow.

Our biggest gratitude goes to all the authors for having provided their chapters to such tight deadlines and participating so enthusiastically. As mentioned, the authors presented their initial thoughts on their respective chapters at a conference at Birkbeck College in January 2000 and we are grateful to the sponsors of that conference, the Football Trust, Cobbetts Solicitors, the Professional Footballers' Association, the British Academy, the Co-operative Party, Waterstones bookshop and Birkbeck College for their support. Many others assisted in making that conference a huge success and our thanks go to Peter Lee and Alastair Bennett at the Football Trust (now Football Foundation); Philip French, then at the Football Trust and now at the Premier League; Peter Hunt, Jean Whitehead and Fay Tinnion at the Co-operative Party; Gordon Taylor at the Professional Footballers' Association; David Dunn at the Co-operative Bank, Tony Clarke MP, Kevin Heath and Malcolm Niekirk at Lester Aldridge Solicitors; and also Jeanette Findlay, Lee Shailer, Jacqueline Mitchell, Stephen Parrott, Roland Muri, Jon Wilson, Simon Rundle, Malini Thakurta, Chukemeka Ajogbe, Claudia Kogler, Roger Brierley, Simon Roberts, Jenny Piesse, Joann McLaughlin, Paula Maris, Peter Trim, Yamg-Im Lee, Jenny Cook, Sally Bland, Oliver Houston, Shonagh Wilkie, Ahmed Thorlu-Bangura, Dave Fenton, Ricky King, Miles A. Van Spall and Paul Windridge for their assistance and participation. We would also like to thank all those who attended the conference, unfortunately too numerous to list here.

We are grateful to Frank Cass & Co. Ltd for their professional work in publishing this book. The staff there have been incredibly helpful in turning the manuscript round with such speed and efficiency and we are particularly grateful to Frank Cass and Jonathan Manley.

This book is about the establishment of Supporters Direct, and particular acknowledgement must be paid to those who have been instrumental in the development and formation of Supporters Direct: Alastair Bennett, Bob Booker, Adam Brown, Andy Burnham, David Dunn, Philip French, Peter Hunt, Kevin Jaquiss, Brian Lomax, Chris Smith and Trevor Watkins. Supporters Direct is now open as a national unit advising supporters on how to become more involved in their clubs, based at Birkbeck College.[6] Without the commitment, vision and energy of this group of people, Supporters Direct simply would not exist.

We were particularly pleased that Johan Cruyff agreed to write a foreword to our last book, *Football in the Digital Age*, in which he wrote of the importance of local community involvement in football clubs. For this book we are honoured that the manager of the most successful football club in Britain, Sir Alex

Ferguson, has agreed to contribute a foreword. Sir Alex writes that even when clubs are as successful on and off the pitch as at Manchester United, they can still ill-afford to exclude their supporters from close involvement in the game. Such an endorsement of the themes of this book from the most successful football manager in recent times underlines the importance of supporter involvement in football clubs and the link between football clubs and their local communities.

Finally, special thanks from Jonathan Michie goes with love to Carloyn, Alex and Duncan. Special thanks from Steven Warby go with love to Jennifer McConnell.

NOTES

1. S. Hamil, J. Michie and C. Oughton (eds.), *A Game of Two Halves? The Business of Football* (Edinburgh: Mainstream, 1999).
2. S. Hamil, J. Michie, C. Oughton and S. Warby (eds.), *Football in the Digital Age: Whose Game Is it Anyway?* (Edinburgh: Mainstream, 2000).
3. See http://www.football-research.org.
4. Football Task Force, *Investing in the Community* (London: Stationery Office, 1999) and *Football: Commercial Issues* (London: Stationery Office, 1999).
5. For further details see the chapters in this volume by Brian Lomax.
6. Supporters Direct can be contacted on 020 7631 6740 (tel) or 020 7631 6872 (fax) or at enquiries@supporters-direct.org. Also see http://www.supporters-direct.org.

1

Recent Developments in Football Ownership

SEAN HAMIL, JONATHAN MICHIE, CHRISTINE OUGHTON and STEVEN WARBY

Over the past decade there have been dramatic changes in the way football is organized as witnessed by the formation of the Premier League, the introduction of all-seater stadiums, the increasing money from TV deals, the dramatic increase in the price of tickets, the transformation of clubs into Plcs, and the growing media ownership of football clubs. Against this background of change one fact remains constant – football clubs need supporters if they are to survive and flourish. Supporters play a vital role not just by turning up and lifting their team's spirits when they are down, but often by providing financial support to buy players or simply by providing funds to keep their club going. The financial backing of supporters over and above the money they spend on tickets and merchandise may be superfluous at a large club like Manchester United, but history is replete with examples of clubs that would have failed but for the financial contributions and commitment of their supporters. Many examples of such cases will be found throughout this volume.

The central theme of this collection is that the positive role that supporters play in football needs to be recognized and harnessed in formal mechanisms that allow supporters a greater say in how their clubs are run. This is particularly important in an era where clubs face financial incentives and pressures from broadcasting deals, redevelopment deals, institutional shareholders and media companies. Faced with such pressures, there is a danger that football might develop in ways that serve the interests of those outside the game and weaken the links between football clubs, supporters and their local communities. Formalizing the positive role that supporters play in football through the creation of *supporters' trusts* is one way of guarding against this danger. This volume explains the development of this line of thinking through the work of the Football Task Force,[1] the publication of the Co-operative Party's pamphlet – *New Mutualism: A Golden Goal?* – and three conferences held at Birkbeck College between February 1999 and January 2000.[2] As a result of this work the government has given its backing to the formation of Supporters Direct – a unit designed to offer legal and practical advice to groups of supporters who wish to form a trust in order to have more say in how their club is run. The second part of this volume shows how these ideas work in practice by providing case studies of supporter involvement and representation at a number of clubs.

The aim of this introductory essay is to place the various contributions and the analyses in the pieces that follow within the context of recent developments in football. Football clubs have always had to balance the need to generate success on the field and the need to stay financially viable through proper organization and management of the business side of the club. The extent to which clubs have managed to satisfy this dual objective is mixed. There is no doubt that a small number of clubs are flourishing in financial terms, but for a variety of reasons many clubs operate on the borderline of viability. The extent to which this is due to poor financial management or poor football management and team performance, or both, differs from club to club, but it is fair to say that inadequate, and in some cases fraudulent business management practices, have played a part. This was one of the conclusions of Lord Justice Taylor's report on the Hillsborough Stadium Disaster which also dealt with the business management of football clubs. When discussing the business management style and motivation of football club directors, Lord Justice Taylor wrote:

> As for the clubs, in some instances it is legitimate to wonder whether the directors are genuinely interested in the welfare of their grassroots supporters. Boardroom struggles for power, wheeler-dealing in the buying and selling of shares and indeed of whole clubs sometimes suggests that those involved are more interested in the personal financial benefits or social status of being a director than of directing the club in the interests of its supporter customers.[3]

Unlike other spheres of business, football is peculiarly vulnerable to exploitation of its customer base because of the loyalty and commitment of its supporters. When the services that a club provides to its customers (supporters) are sub-standard, most supporters feel they have no choice but to carry on supporting their club. In almost all other spheres of business, sub-standard products would make customers shop elsewhere. It is ironic, but nonetheless true, that the lifeblood of clubs – the supporters – are often treated so badly because they show such loyalty.

The incentive to run the business side of football clubs in a way that is detrimental to both the sporting and cultural interests of a club, and the interests of supporters and local communities, has always been present. It was in order to curb this threat that early in the game's history the Football Association (FA) introduced Rule 34 which prevented directors from extracting significant income and profits from the clubs they ran. However, in the 1990s the FA sanctioned the bypassing of this rule by permitting clubs to form holding companies which were floated on the stock market as Plcs. The stock market flotation of football clubs has magnified the potential conflict of interest between the business and sporting side of a football club's activity, as the final report of the Football Task Force

2

makes clear, '...[many] supporters who have bought shares in their football club, usually through an act of loyalty, have seen the value of their shares fall dramatically. This has often happened at the same time as clubs have increased their prices, thus creating a two-fold burden on the supporter.'[4]

Stock market flotation has meant that clubs take (undue) account of the interests of shareholders who have bought shares purely as a financial investment whilst ignoring the interests of supporter shareholders. The interests of non-supporter shareholders are often diametrically opposed to those of supporter shareholders. For example, financial investors have an interest in higher ticket prices, while supporter shareholders have an interest in keeping ticket prices affordable. Financial investors will sell their shares if their demands for a financial return are not met, while supporter shareholders are unlikely to part with what they see as a stake in their club. In the absence of any mechanism for supporter involvement, it is not difficult to see who is likely to lose out from this inherent conflict of interest. Supporter shareholders are unlikely to sell their shares and unlikely to give up their season tickets: they bear the cost of falling share prices and higher ticket prices. This happens despite the fact that the proportion of shares held by supporters is often equal to that of large institutional investors with whom the club would regularly consult. However, the diffuse ownership of shares by supporters means that their voice is not heard notwithstanding the fact that their *collective* ownership is large enough to warrant a dialogue with directors or a place on the board.

The stock market flotation of football clubs has also opened up a further potential source of conflict as it has paved the way for media ownership and control of many clubs. Media companies – predominantly BSkyB and NTL – now have ownership stakes in nine out of the 20 Premier League clubs. However, as the Monopolies and Mergers Commission (MMC) report into the proposed take-over of Manchester United by BSkyB made clear, media company ownership of football clubs raises public interest concerns. These concerns arise not only through the detrimental effect of media ownership on competition in the broadcasting industry but also through the likely adverse effects on the organization of football, the inequality between the richest and poorest clubs and resultant negative effects on the overall quality of the English game. As Nicholas Finney, a member of the Monopolies and Mergers Commission's panel, wrote in *Football in the Digital Age*:

> BSkyB continued to make a heartfelt plea which focused on how the importance of football to its viewing profile would mean that it would never do anything which might be regarded as detrimental to the game. However, once again, the panel concluded that by increasing BSkyB's influence over the Premier League's decisions, the merger could lead to a situation whereby some decisions taken would not be in the long-term interests of football, giving rise to the adverse effect that the quality of British football would be damaged.[5]

For a variety of reasons, as explained in Peter Crowther's study, media companies have limited their ownership stakes in football clubs to less than 10 per cent of the total value of shares. Despite this, most of the ownership deals give the media companies explicit rights and control over important parts of the way the clubs are run. At the same time, the voice of supporters who often collectively own similar stakes in their clubs is ignored.

The Football Task Force report on *Football: Commercial Issues* (the majority report) argues that media ownership of football clubs

> i) threatens fair competition, raising similar concerns to those raised by the MMC in rejecting the BSkyB/Manchester United take-over; (ii) in some instances transgresses Premier League, FA and Football League rules governing joint ownership of clubs; iii) threatens the collective sale of television rights and the redistribution of that income which the whole Task Force has endorsed in our third report.[6]

To remedy this situation the Task Force recommended that 'the Department of Trade and Industry should publish guidelines on mergers involving football clubs which takes account of their particular market conditions, in its continuing development of rules governing competition and the public interest in relation to football clubs'.[7] These guidelines should ensure that all clubs be subject to referral under competition law on mergers and take-overs to protect supporters against public interest concerns arising from ownership of football clubs by media companies.

In addition, the Task Force recommended that clubs intending to float on the stock market, or sell their stadiums for redevelopment should consult with all sections of supporters and show that the flotation is in the long term interests of the club. In terms of supporter involvement in football clubs, the Football Task Force 'majority report' recommended that supporters should be given more say in how their clubs are run. In addition the report recommended that the government should 'encourage communities, through local councils, to take an equity stake in their club'.[8]

At the time of writing, the Task Force's final report is still under consideration by the Minister for Sport but in the meantime the government has announced its backing for the formation of Supporters Direct, a dedicated unit that will provide legal and practical advice to help supporters form supporter trusts and gain a say in running their clubs.

The creation of Supporters Direct and the formation of supporters' trusts constitute an effective bottom–up mechanism for making clubs more accountable to widespread public interest concerns. At the same time the Football Task Force majority report has recommended stronger regulation of football through the creation of a Football Audit Commission and a Code of Practice as discussed below. Together these two forms of regulation should do much to ensure the future health of the game and resolve inherent conflicts between the commercial and business interests of football clubs on the one hand, and the wider cultural and sporting interests of clubs, their supporters and local communities on the other.

PART 1 – SETTING THE SCENE: THE GENESIS OF SUPPORTERS DIRECT

Part 1 of this volume opens with a piece by Chris Smith MP, the Minister for Culture, Media and Sport, that sets out the Government's proposals for the formation of Supporters Direct. He begins by painting two possible scenarios for the future development of the game. The first sees an unfettered continuation of recent trends towards greater inequality between the richest and poorest clubs, inflation in ticket prices, decline in grass-roots football facilities and over-development of the television coverage of the game resulting in a shift in the nature of support away from attendance at matches to more TV viewing. As a consequence, there will be a dwindling in football crowds, bankruptcy of a number of smaller clubs and eventually a reduction in TV viewing audiences as the game is overexposed and matches become less exciting due to a combination of the lack of competitive balance between clubs and the absence of a packed crowd which detracts from the attractiveness of televised matches.

The alternative scenario is to foster a competitive English league by promoting greater equality, strengthening grass-roots football and taking steps to encourage attendance at football grounds through differential ticket pricing that guards against social exclusion. Under this scenario clubs would be run in a business–like fashion which takes account of the views of their customers – the supporters.

The main argument of this essay is that the second scenario requires all those in the game to work together to achieve it – the football authorities, government and supporters. Greater involvement of supporters is central to this task:

> Football supporters hold the key to football's future. They are the game's greatest asset, the people who pay the ticket prices, TV subscriptions and buy the merchandise. They keep the game in business. Where clubs have been in crisis, they have more often than not been saved by their supporters – and emerged all the stronger for it. The more enlightened clubs know it is in their commercial interest to value their supporters and involve them in the affairs of the clubs – not see them as 'turnstile-fodder' who can be expected to turn up week after week regardless of the quality of the product.[9]

The government aims to encourage supporter involvement in football clubs through the establishment of its new initiative Supporters Direct. Supporters Direct became fully operational before the start of the 2000–2001 season, providing legal and practical support for supporters to form supporters' trusts with a view to be actively involved in the way their clubs are run.

The third essay, by Brian Lomax – the first elected director at Northampton Town FC and a director of Supporters Direct, explains the genesis and principles of the government's new initiative, from the Task Force's *Investing in the Community* report published in January 1999, to the launch of Supporters Direct in August 2000. Supporters Direct is grounded in three principles: influence, ownership and representation. As Brian explains, in order to be eligible for assistance from Supporters Direct supporters' groups must have democratic structures that are open to all fans and representative of a broad range of supporters. Once these criteria are met groups will be eligible for a package of legal, practical and financial advice. An important part of this work will be to provide legal blueprints for the organization and operation of supporters' trusts that meet the needs of individual clubs. To this end Supporters Direct will deal with individual supporters' groups and run conferences, seminars and training courses. At the time of writing, nine trusts have been formed already and a further five agreed.

Trevor Brooking CBE, Chairman of Sport England provides an endorsement of the aims and objectives of Supporters Direct and shows how this initiative dovetails with the work of Sport England. He explains how the role of clubs in their local community must be encouraged in order to increase interest and participation in football and sport more generally – facilitating supporter involvement in football clubs is an important part of this task. Trevor describes how as a boy his experience of feeling a part of the club he supported – West Ham – and building a rapport with the players, encouraged him to embark on a career in professional football. One of the key objectives of Sport England is to increase the numbers of people who are involved and participating in sport. As Trevor writes, 'football can promote social interaction and inclusion', and the work of Supporters Direct complements that of Sport England in its objective to involve more people in sport.

Peter Crowther, an expert in competition law at Rosenblatt's Solicitors, explores the grounds for intervention by the competition authorities to protect against the public interest concerns raised by media control of football clubs. The expansion of the pay-TV market has increased the amount of money flowing into football and opened up new opportunities. At the same time, it is evident that media companies have specific interests in football that require regulatory intervention in order to ensure fair competition in broadcasting, preserve the quality of football and prevent the exploitation of consumers, in this case, football supporters.[10] If the new opportunities arising from increasing flows of money coming into the game are to be taken, careful and proper regulation is required. Such regulation can take two forms. First, supporters can and should be given a greater say in how their clubs are run, which is the central theme of this volume. This might provide beneficial countervailing power to the influence of media companies. Second, there needs to be adequate regulation and control of media control and ownership of football clubs via competition law. This essay is concerned with recent developments in media ownership of football clubs and the grounds for intervention by the regulatory authorities.

Richard Faulkner presents the findings of the Football Task Force from his perspective as Deputy Chair. In doing so, he gives the overall context from which the issue of supporter involvement in football clubs emerged onto the public agenda. Lord Faulkner describes the Task Force's remit and outlines the consultative processes involved in its work, and argues that the Task Force was successful in meeting its primary objectives. He describes how the Task Force quantified the level of supporter dissatisfaction with football, giving the reasons for its recommendations. He also gives his perspective on the rationale behind the presentation of differing 'minority' and 'majority' versions of the Task Force's final report, and makes a powerful argument for the adoption of the 'majority' report recommendations, including supporting the establishment of supporters' trusts and Supporters Direct.

In addition to the suggestions regarding supporter involvement, an important recommendation of the majority report was the establishment of a Football Audit Commission and detailed Code of Practice to implement the report's recommendations with the proviso that, if after a period of two years there was insufficient progress towards implementing the recommendations, the Minister for Culture, Media and Sport should appoint an independent statutory body to regulate the football industry.

Taken together the pieces by Peter Crowther and Lord Faulkner also make the case for the need for both top-down regulation by the competition authorities and the football authorities, and bottom-up regulation via greater supporter involvement in football clubs if football is to develop along the lines of the second scenario outlined by Chris Smith.

Andy Burnham, drawing on his experience as a former administrator for the Football Task Force, describes how the typical relationship between supporters' groups and football club owners and administrators had become characterized by distrust. He outlines how the net consequence of this legacy was negative for clubs and offers examples of how clubs which have adopted a conciliatory partnership towards their supporters' organizations have benefited considerably. He also challenges the conception commonly held by club administrators that supporters' groups can neither muster the expertise nor conduct themselves with the discretion required to make an effective contribution to the running of their clubs. He argues that, as has been demonstrated by the many benefits which have flowed from the Football Task Force exercise, Supporters Direct may have a major contribution to make in facilitating the synergy between supporters' groups and club administrators to unlock substantial benefits for both parties.

PART 2: SUPPORTERS' TRUSTS IN ACTION

Part 2 of this volume aims to show how the ideas outlined in Part 1 work in practice, and to give case-studies of supporter involvement and representation at a number of football clubs. Kevin Jaquiss, a leading lawyer who specializes in models of mutuality for corporate governance, describes the various legal models that supporters' trusts might take. He draws on the example of the Crystal Palace Supporters' Trust and describes its efforts to save the club and seek effective supporter representation. Kevin is also legal adviser to the Government-backed Supporters Direct initiative, and he outlines the democratic, mutual and not for profit legal structures Supporters Direct has developed. These include companies limited by guarantee, industrial and provident societies and trusts. Jaquiss thus gives an expert analysis of the technical issues involved in establishing vehicles for greater supporter involvement in football clubs.

In the ninth essay, one of the leading figures behind Supporters Direct, and Chairman of AFC Bournemouth, Trevor Watkins, writes of his experience as an ordinary fan who went on to become Chairman of the club he supported. He describes how he and a group of colleagues led the campaign to save AFC Bournemouth from financial ruin and raised enough money to buy the club with the help of a Community Trust. Trevor describes the pitfalls and skills necessary for any group of fans contemplating an active role in club management, and makes a powerful case for other clubs to take the issue of supporter involvement on board.

Michael Crick, journalist, broadcaster and author, shows that it is not just the supporters of small, lower league clubs who are seeking greater representation and involvement in football with his account of the activities of shareholding Manchester United supporters, Shareholders United. He describes how this evolved from a group of supporters who came together to campaign against the proposed take-over of Manchester United by BSkyB into a fully fledged supporter-shareholder organization seeking wider share ownership among supporters and representation of this group's interests to the club. Michael details successes and difficulties with establishing working relations with the club, and concludes that organizations such as Shareholders United have a vital role to play as part of the checks and balances needed in an era of increasing commercialization in football.

Peter Carr, Jeanette Findlay, Sean Hamil, Joe Hill and Stephen Morrow, all founder members of the supporter-shareholder organization at Glasgow Celtic – The Celtic Trust – outline the genesis of the organization. They describe how the roots of the club as a charitable self-help organization led to the establishment of such an endeavour. They then illustrate how the decision of Fergus McCann, the former owner of a controlling interest in Celtic, to sell his shares to existing supporter-shareholders and season-ticket holders has created a window of opportunity for supporters who wish to exercise more influence over how the club is administered. They detail the progress of the trust, the obstacles overcome, and conclude by presenting a detailed outlined of the Celtic Trust 'Statement of Principles' document on which the formal constitution of the organization, which was registered as an Industrial & Provident Society in August 2000, was based.

Adam Brown and Andy Walsh, both of whom have been heavily involved in various football supporter campaigns in the UK, put supporter involvement in football clubs in its wider European context by charting the extent of fan representation and participation in Italy, Spain and Germany. They analyse supporter involvement in these countries in the differing overall context of the historical role of supporters' organizations, how European football clubs are organized and run, and the differing issues of access. They describe the activities of the *ultras* in Italy, club membership organizations such as L'Elefant Blau in Spain, and supporters' reactions to the more cautious approach to commercialism taken by football clubs in Germany. Although they find it difficult to draw direct comparisons, the authors suggest that pressures on the game similar to those in the UK (that is, effects of the *Bosman* ruling, increases in expenditure, the role of media companies, and so on) may produce greater politicization of supporter organizations across the continent.

Taken together, these contributions represent a thorough and authoritative call to those charged with the future direction of football. Each of the authors represented here argues convincingly that football can reap the benefits of increased commercialization whilst still remaining the people's game. The historical bonds between football clubs, their local communities and their loyal supporters need not be swept away by global market forces. Everyone agrees that football is flourishing at the moment; record sums of money are being pumped into the game, foreign stars are eager to play in the UK and audiences are at record levels. But for football to flourish and have longevity, this success must be built on solid foundations. Football has the opportunity to bring in and benefit from the involvement of its supporters. A football club that ignores the loyalty of its solid support does so at its peril.

NOTES

1. The Football Task Force, *Football: Commercial Issues* (London: Stationery Office, 1999), p.36.
2. J. Michie, *New Mutualism: A Golden Goal? Uniting Supporters and Their Clubs* (London: The Co-operative Party, 1999), available from The Co-operative Party, 77 Weston Street, London SE1 3SD, telephone 020 7357 0230, fax 020 7407 4476, e-mail d.jones@co-op-party.org.uk.
3. Lord Justice Taylor (Chairman), *Inquiry into the Hillsborough Stadium Disaster: Final Report*, Cmnd 962 (London: HMSO, 1990), Paragraph 53.
4. The Football Task Force, *Football: Commercial Issues*, p.36.
5. N. Finney, 'The MMC's Inquiry into BSkyB's Merger with Manchester United plc', in S. Hamil, J. Michie, C. Oughton and S. Warby (eds.), *Football in the Digital Age: Whose Game Is it Anyway?* (Edinburgh: Mainstream, 2000), pp.79–80.

 6. The Football Task Force, *Football: Commercial Issues*, p.39.
 7. Ibid., p.39.
 8. Ibid.
 9. See Chris Smith, Minister for Culture, Media and Sport, in this volume p.14.
10. Monopolies and Mergers Commission, *British Sky Broadcasting plc and Manchester United plc: A Report on the Proposed Merger* (London: Stationery Office, 1999).

PART 1

Setting the Scene:
The Genesis of Supporters Direct

2

Strengthening the Voice of Supporters

CHRIS SMITH MP

What should we make of football in the 1990s now we are able to look back? It was without doubt a decade of great change for English football, coming out of the pain and horror of the Hillsborough disaster. The televising of the game changed the business of football forever and brought unprecedented wealth. Millions of pounds – from public and private sources – were invested in improving stadiums and developing new academies and centres of excellence. Problems that scarred the game in the 1980s diminished: violence around matches became less common and incidents of racism – arguably at a peak at the end of the 1980s – became more isolated.

At the end of the decade, crowds were healthier and more diverse than at any other time in the game's history, with more women and families attending matches. But, despite all these positives, the 1990s saw the emergence of a new set of problems for football.

First, we saw the financial divide between football's elite and medium to smaller size clubs become gradually wider. By the end of the 1997/98 season, over 80 per cent of clubs in the Premier League were generating an operating profit but the same percentage of clubs in the three divisions of the Football League were making an operating loss.

Second, and this is linked to the first, the country's major domestic honours came to be dominated by a handful of big clubs while, at the other end of the table, we saw the emergence of a band of so-called 'yo-yo' clubs. The 1999/2000 Premiership season was arguably the least competitive and most predictable to date.

Third, we saw huge inflation in the cost of supporting football, with many people on lower incomes now unable to afford to attend matches. Other commercial issues came into sharp focus, such as the merchandising of replica kits and the flotation of clubs on the stock market.

Finally, despite all the wealth in the top of the game, we saw the continued decline of the standard of playing facilities at the game's true grassroots – in the schools and parks.

So what shape do we expect football to be in at the end of 2010, with the way things are going? I can see two futures. If the game carries along the same path in the next ten years as it did in the nineties, the chances are that the top league will have become more divided and even less competitive. Coupled with continued above-inflation ticket prices increases, this would lead to dwindling interest and fall-off in crowds. Games played in empty grounds make a less good television spectacle so TV audiences may have started to decline too. A number of clubs in the lower divisions will most probably have folded.

Or football could go down another route. My vision for football at the end of this decade would be to have a strong, competitive English league, underpinned by a vibrant and healthy grass-roots structure extending right down to primary schools, and a strong girls' and women's game. This would give England the greatest chance of success in international football. I would want to see healthy attendances at football, with nobody excluded by price, and clubs run in a business-like way with supporters consulted and involved. Is this too optimistic? I do not believe that it is. But to realize the vision, we will have to work at it. That means football authorities, government and supporters – in fact everybody who cares about and takes an interest in the game.

Football supporters hold the key to football's future. They are the game's greatest asset, the people who pay the ticket prices, TV subscriptions and buy the merchandise. They keep the game in business. Where clubs have been in crisis, they have more often than not been saved by their supporters – and emerged all the stronger for it. The more enlightened clubs know it is in their commercial interest to value their supporters and involve them in the affairs of the clubs – not see them as 'turnstile-fodder' who can be expected to turn up week after week regardless of the quality of the product.

That is the simple philosophy of Supporters Direct – the new initiative I announced at the 1999 Labour Party Conference to help supporters achieve a say in the future of their clubs, including where appropriate the provision of legal and other advice to supporter groups who wish to set up mutual trusts and raise resources to invest in their clubs. Less than a year after my initial announcement, Supporters Direct became fully operational – in time for the 2000/2001 football season.

Supporters Direct recognizes that the vast majority of supporters see clubs as cherished community assets, built on generations of support from families. It also recognizes that clubs in the lower divisions cannot sustain losses year after year and that the time has come to look at new ways of helping them onto a firmer financial footing.

I hope people involved in all aspects of football will see Supporters Direct as an opportunity, not a threat. It is an opportunity to forge a new relationship between supporters, their clubs and the local community. To give clubs a more solid financial base and supporters a proper say in return for the financial support that they plough in year after year.

Government thinking on this issue was inspired by the 1999 Co-operative Party's pamphlet *New Mutualism: A Golden Goal?* written by Professor Jonathan Michie.[1] The ideas in the pamphlet are based on the same core values as the Labour movement – community self-help, mutual support, social responsibility; that we achieve more together than we do alone.

The tremendous response we have already received to the idea of Supporters Direct suggests that this is an idea for which the time has come. It clearly has direct resonance and appeal to supporters across the country. By August 2000 the newly established Supporters Direct unit had received over 50 firm expressions of interest from supporters from a wide range of clubs – Division Three up to the Premier League. A major county cricket club and several rugby league clubs have also been in touch and I see no reason why these ideas should not be applied to sports other than football.

My announcement in October 1999 set out my aim of securing a source of professional and accessible advice to supporters in looking towards a greater involvement in the running of their football club. As many supporters will know from direct personal experience – and others will learn from the other contributions to this volume – there are many complex issues that supporters need to address in order to secure greater involvement in their club – whether ownership of the club is in private hands or already public as a plc.

Supporters Direct aims to offer practical help to supporters' groups interested in taking a financial stake in their clubs – and as a result gaining a greater say in its affairs – through the setting up of a supporters' trust. In most cases, this will involve basic legal advice, sharing experience and modest help with start-up costs. The Co-operative Bank has separately agreed to offer preferential banking to supporters' trusts.

Of course, supporters' trusts will not be the solution for every football club and I do not want Government to lay down a blueprint for the administration of football clubs. It is for sports clubs to look after their own affairs. This initiative is not about being prescriptive or foisting solutions on to clubs. Indeed the establishment of a trust in clubs whose shares are not listed on the Stock Exchange may only prove possible with the club's consent. Co-operation between the supporters' trust and the club is also important since in almost every case supporters will only be able to take a minority stake and so will need to work with other shareholders.

However, it is a matter of concern for politicians if fans feel consistently excluded from the affairs of their club or sport and believe their interests both as consumers as well as supporters are not being looked after. That is why I want the best possible advice to be provided to those seeking to establish supporters' trusts.

Not only am I keen to ensure that supporters get the best possible advice when seeking to establish trusts, but also that such advice draws on the experience of those who have already successfully secured greater involvement in their clubs so that solutions to the particular difficulties relating to football clubs are not reinvented in different parts of the country. I asked the Football Trust to call together a working group to advise me on how best such advice could be delivered to those who need it and what form that advice should take.

It is inevitable that it takes some time for these sorts of detail to be worked out in such a complex area but within just a few months we succeeded in developing concrete proposals. I should like to pay tribute to that working group under the chairmanship of Brian Lomax, Britain's first supporter-elected director in League football. Jonathan Michie at Birkbeck, and Trevor Watkins, Chairman of AFC Bournemouth, also both played key roles in that working group, and the group was ably assisted by the officials of the Football Trust, in particular Philip French and Alastair Bennett. Recognition is also due to Peter Hunt of the Co-operative Party who has helped bring these ideas to fruition through the timely publication of the pamphlet.

I intend that any advice coming from Supporters Direct should be impartial and free from influence from any quarter. It is my hope that Supporters Direct will have the scope both to offer advice on one-off issues and to play a supporting role to those going through the various steps of establishing supporters' trusts. Its work will include the provision of model trust deeds and constitutions to be used in the formation of supporters' trusts; help with legal and/or financial advice; and the provision of training and networking for those involved in the work of supporters' trusts.

It is essential that any supporters' organization is truly representative of all the fans it seeks to represent and that its administration is open and democratic. Indeed, Supporters Direct has quite rightly made it a requirement for any organization seeking advice from the new Unit that it meets these criteria.

I hope that any football supporter who has turned to this volume in the hope that – together with their fellow supporters – they will be able to gain a greater say in the life of the football club they support, will have found the various contributions informative and productive. I hope too that it will represent the start of the final lap in the journey towards securing a strengthened voice for supporters in football.

NOTE

1. J. Michie, *New Mutualism: A Golden Goal? Uniting Supporters and Their Clubs* (London: The Co-operative Party, 1999), available from The Co-operative Party, 77 Weston Street, London SE1 3SD, telephone 020 7357 0230, fax 020 7407 4476, e-mail d.jones@co-op-party.org.uk.

3

Episode One:
May the Force Be with You!

BRIAN LOMAX

We were all indebted to Adam Brown for his detailed account of the work and tribulations of the Football Task Force in *A Game of Two Halves? The Business of Football.*[1] Unfortunately, due to publishing deadlines, his story remained unfinished. It is necessary to refer to subsequent events in order to understand the birth pangs of Supporters Direct.

At the first Regional Meeting of the Task Force at Filbert Street, Leicester, on 22 January 1998, I had a very fair hearing from their Working Group. I had gone there to represent Northampton Town Supporters' Trust (as Chair) and Northampton Town Football Club (as the supporters' elected Director). Because these two meetings were an hour apart, I was invited to remain for the intervening meeting with Local Authority representatives, including Councillor Les Patterson of Northampton Borough Council, and to participate. It was thus possible to present to the Task Force a clear picture of the three-way partnership which we had developed in Northampton between the Football Club, the Supporters' Trust and the Local Authority which had breathed new life into Northampton Town FC.[2]

This was the start of a long and, for me, enlightening relationship with the Task Force. In their first two reports, dealing with issues of racism[3] and disability[4] in football, generous acknowledgement was given to the landmark achievements at Northampton. In 1996 we had become the first professional Football Club to adopt an Equal Opportunities Policy, and had been in the forefront of the 'Kick It Out' campaign before and since. We had also won in 1997 the national McDonald's Award for the best facilities and services for disabled supporters in British football, ahead of all Premiership clubs both sides of the border. All this and much more had been achieved as a result of the three-way partnership referred to above.

When the Task Force turned to the more contentious issues in its remit, the cracks began to appear in its surface. By the time its third report appeared,[5] Gordon Taylor of the Professional Footballers' Association had resigned (though he appointed a substitute as an observer) and had made public his reasons for doing so. I was to learn later that Trustees led by Tom Pendry MP had attempted to remove working facilities at the Football Trust offices from the Task Force staff, and had written to the Secretary of State about this. Although their attempt failed, the episode made it increasingly difficult for the staff to continue their work productively, and fomented an atmosphere of discord which only increased for the remainder of the Task Force's life. At the same time, the Task Force's grossly inadequate budget of £100,000 ran out, and when its Administrator, Andy Burnham, left weeks later to take up a position in the Department of Culture, Media and Sport (DCMS), there was no money left to appoint or pay a successor. We then witnessed the unedifying spectacle of a public body, from which the Government had derived immense kudos and publicity, relying on the services of David Mahoney, an excellent but unpaid young graduate on work experience, unofficially assisted in his spare time by Philip French, Head of Communications of the Football Trust, who himself was forced to resign from the Task Force on more than one occasion. Intense lobbying from the few who knew the true situation eventually elicited a small additional sum, enabling David Mahoney to be paid until he went to law school, but when he left he was not replaced, and the working secretariat of the Task Force devolved upon Philip French and Sue O'Brien in addition to their full-time jobs with the Trust.

'Investing in the Community', launched in the marshland which passes for football facilities behind HMP Wormwood Scrubs, proved a landmark event for the Task Force, the conception of Supporters Direct, and it was hoped, the starting-point for the systematic redistribution of some of football's immense wealth to the have-nots. This had, of course, been the historic role of the Football Association, equally historically abandoned in 1992 with the birth of the breakaway FA Premier League. In a superb piece of negotiation, Andy Burnham and Philip French had persuaded the Premier League to pledge 5 per cent of the revenue from the next and subsequent televised rights agreements to the grassroots of the game. Countless thousands of youngsters and amateur players, who may never know their names, will have cause to be grateful to Burnham and French in years to come. I dedicate this essay to them.

The Task Force report *Investing in the Community* also continued the development at national level of the ideas we had initiated at Northampton in 1991/92,[6] and noted that:

> A club should not have to be on the brink of collapse before developments such as these can happen. There is a strong case for financial support being made available as a means of encouraging more supporters groups to establish trusts and become involved in the running of their clubs. We believe that this represents a new model of ownership for all football clubs, but particularly small clubs, into the next Millennium.[7]

This paragraph was the first seed of Supporters Direct.

It was to be nearly a year and many drafts later that the fourth and final report of the Task Force emerged.[8] Known popularly as 'The Commercial Report', it was in fact entitled *Football: Commercial Issues*, and was perhaps better known for the disagreements surrounding it than for its contents. It was in fact two reports, majority and minority, the problem being that the minority consisted of most of the major cash-holders in the industry.

Clearly these major powers – the FA, the FA Premier League, and the Football League – were anxious to minimize any concession of their power, whether to Government, fans, an independent regulator, or anybody else. Their minority report was framed accordingly. At the time of writing, Government is still deliberating between the two sets of proposals.

The majority report enjoyed the support of, among others, both national supporters' organizations and all the academic and independent members of the Task Force. I would here draw particular attention to chapter 7, entitled 'Supporter Involvement'. Having described in some detail the background to the Northampton example, as it had by now become known, the report goes on to say, 'Supporter representation has an important part to play in achieving a balance between legitimate commercial ambitions and football clubs' role as public institutions. The Task Force concurs with Brian Lomax's view that supporter representation must be "democratic, affordable, entrenched and independent".'[9] Warming to the theme, the report continues:

> The situation at many clubs already is that supporters, taken as a whole, own a substantial proportion of shares in a club. The Task Force believes that the clubs should give much more recognition to this and that supporter shareholders should be encouraged to collectivise their shares into a voting block. This group could then elect a representative to the Board. Additionally, according to company law, a ten per cent stakeholding would allow a supporters trust to call an Extraordinary General Meeting in the event of supporter/club conflict.[10]

This, of course, refers to existing shareholders and those with the purchasing power to become shareholders in their own right. But mindful of its previous point about affordability, the report goes on to say: 'Many supporters are investigating the possibilities of trusts at their clubs, in which shares are held collectively and protected in perpetuity. We believe that this is a desirable development and recommend that the FA, the FAC and the clubs encourage democratic, independent, organised and financially entrenched supporter representation.' Thus in its fourth and final report, the Task Force put flesh on the bones of the seminal proposal in *Investing in the Community*. By then, of course, Chris Smith, the Secretary of State for Culture, Media and Sport, had announced the impending formation of Supporters Direct at the Labour Party Conference in October 1999.[11]

The Commercial Report was published on 22 December 1999, some members doubtless hoping that it would get lost in the Christmas post or at least achieve minimal media coverage over the festive season. However, Christmas was not long over when Chris Smith launched Supporters Direct in much more specific terms, at the Conference 'Supporter Involvement in Football Clubs' at Birkbeck College, University of London, on 27 January 2000.

The Core Working Group of Supporters Direct consisted of Professor Jonathan Michie of Birkbeck College, Trevor Watkins, Chairman of AFC Bournemouth, and myself, working in association with Alastair Bennett and Philip French of the Football Trust. The three of us had first been called together, without prior knowledge of the proposal, by Peter Hunt to address a fringe meeting at the 1999 Labour Party Conference. The meeting was organized by the Co-operative Party of which Peter is the National Secretary. He played a major part in brokering the proposal of Supporters Direct, in particular the participation of the Co-operative Bank.

The Core Group had been charged with preparing a business plan for the DCMS as a basis for considering an input of public funds. It was at that stage assumed, and even announced by Chris Smith at Birkbeck, that this would be via the Football Foundation, the prospective legal successor of the Football Trust. Supporters Direct had already been accepted and publicized as a constituent part of the Football Trust, and the DCMS expected that this would continue into the Foundation. I was at no stage fully convinced of the desirability of this, and indeed wrote to the DCMS in my covering letter (18 January 2000) to the first draft of our business plan:

> We are anxious to avoid some of the difficulties which beset the Football Task Force ... (including) its physical dependency upon the premises of the Football Trust, which has Trustees representing all major vested interests within the industry, including the Football Association, the Football League, the FA Premier League and the Professional Footballers' Association ... It is likely that Supporters Direct will at some stage of its life be involved in action which may be resented by some of those who currently hold monopoly powers within the industry. The Unit is, after all, about the partial democratization of professional football, and about the transfer of some power in the game from the haves to the have-nots. If the Unit is to operate with integrity according to its Statement of Philosophy and Aims, it needs to have a measure of financial, geographical and academic independence ... We propose that ... the core costs of staffing and running the Unit should be ringfenced and kept free from the control or interference of the vested interests within the industry. We are not seeking to exclude them from our deliberations – in fact we propose an Advisory Committee for the Unit with regular meetings on which they would all be represented – but we feel from the Task Force experience that for them to have management and/or financial control would be detrimental to the work of the Unit.

Chris Smith responded affirmatively to these concerns in his launch address at Birkbeck College nine days later, and indeed went so far as to offer a Government guarantee of protection against interference with Supporters Direct, but all within the context of our membership of the Football Foundation. He also guaranteed that adequate funding would be in place for a start date of 1 April 2000.

There then followed three months of uncertainty before the shadow Board of the Foundation decided whether it wanted Supporters Direct within its ranks. By now the work had begun in earnest, on a voluntary basis. We were overwhelmed at the volume of response to us from supporters' groups, over 50 by the time April came, representing every division of the English and Scottish Leagues (though due to devolution we had no funding for work in Scotland), and a number of non-League clubs. It was soon clear that demand for our services would always exceed the supply of them to which our likely funding would stretch, and that we would need to seek additional financial support from elsewhere.

Despite pressure from the DCMS, the Football Foundation finally decided against adopting us as a constituent body, principally I believe due to the influence of the FA Premier League, the Foundation's major funders. I was neither surprised nor dismayed by this decision. Indeed, following a meeting with Dave Richards, the Premier League's Chairman, and Mike Lee, their spokesperson, I expected it. I was assured by them of a cordial and co-operative relationship, and I believe this will be more healthy than if we had been a subordinate part of the Foundation. Supporters Direct is now therefore based at Birkbeck College.

I will conclude this piece with a description of Supporters Direct and of what we can offer supporters' organizations which seek to work with us. Rightly in my view, the first task the Core Group set itself was to write a Statement of Philosophy and Aims. It reads as follows:

> The aim of Supporters Direct is to offer support, advice and information to groups of supporters who wish to play a responsible part in the life of the clubs they support.
>
> All models used and recommended will be based on democratic, mutual and 'not-for-profit' principles. Legitimate objectives will include:
>
> **Influence** – the formation and running of representative bodies for supporters.
>
> **Ownership** – the acquisition of shares in the football club to pool the voting power of individual supporters to further the aims and objects of the Supporters' Trust.
>
> **Representation** – securing the democratic election of supporters' representatives to the Boards of Directors of individual football clubs.
>
> By these means we hope to improve the health of the whole football industry.

CRITERIA FOR ELIGIBILITY
To qualify for the assistance of Supporters Direct, supporters' groups must be:
Democratic in their structures and in the way they run their affairs;
Open to all fans to join, at an affordable cost; and
Broadly representative of supporters.

This statement set the tone for all the work that followed, and despite further delays, at the time of writing we are set to go, with our headquarters and starter-pack ready, in time for the beginning of the new 2000/2001 season. We have already offered a casework service to dozens of supporters' groups, but now this will be backed by the resources that only funding can bring: national publicity, literature and above all the input of dedicated staff. Although there will be the capacity to offer small seed-corn grants in cases of need, all the evidence thus far tells us that this is a people business and should be labour intensive. The enthusiasm of the groups themselves will in most cases generate the funds and sponsorship necessary to cover start-up costs, provided that the expensive and specialist legal and financial advice can be offered free by Supporters Direct. This we are able to do by an economy of scale, having identified the best available professional resources at the outset. The first task of any new group is, of course, to draft and adopt a Constitution suitable for its needs. A number of alternative models are now available: an unincorporated Trust, a Company Limited by Guarantee, or an Industrial and Provident Society.[12] All have been used, all have their merits, and all are democratic and not-for-profit. We can work with groups as they decide which model is most appropriate to their own local situation, and then provide the relevant documents. All Constitutions should contain the powers to buy and hold shares in the Football Club, and to elect Directors to the Board.

In addition to our own advice and experience, the help of our staff and the legal and financial service, Supporters Direct will be organizing a series of conferences, seminars, training courses and support groups for supporters seeking and taking on positions of responsibility in their Trust or their Football Club. These will be held at various venues throughout the country once we are fully established. We will attend local planning group meetings as required, and will offer speakers for public launch meetings. An e-mail group (supporters-direct@egroups.com) and an official website (http://www.supporters-direct.org) are already active, and regular newsletters will go to all groups on our database. We will also be producing literature for distribution to supporters, and will give advice on how to produce their own.

We regard our close association with the Co-operative Movement as a guarantee of the quality and integrity of our work. They in turn see us as a good example of co-operative and mutual principles in action, and hope thereby to promote these principles nationally to a new generation. What we say and do will not always please everyone, because we are about the redistribution of power in football from the haves to the have-nots. But our message has already been music to the ears of thousands of fans up and down the country – ask them at Aylesbury, Cambridge United, Celtic, Chester, Crystal Palace, Enfield, Leyton Orient, Lincoln, Luton, Southend and Walsall, to name only a few. Before we have received a penny, nine trusts have been formed, another five agreed. Three groups have shareholdings, and six now have elected supporters' representatives on the Board. Come and join us – and may the Force be with you!

NOTES

1. A. Brown, 'Thinking the Unthinkable or Playing the Game? The Football Task Force, New Labour and the Reform of English Football', in S. Hamil, J. Michie and C. Oughton (eds.), *A Game of Two Halves? The Business of Football* (Edinburgh: Mainstream, 1999), pp.56–81.
2. B. Lomax, 'Supporter Representation on the Board', in *A Game of Two Halves?*, pp.195–201.
3. Football Task Force, *Eliminating Racism from Football* (London: Stationery Office, 1998), pp.12, 40, 42.
4. Football Task Force, *Improving Facilities for Disabled Supporters* (London: Stationery Office, 1998), *passim*.
5. Football Task Force, *Investing in the Community* (January 1999).
6. Ibid., pp.39, 44–5.
7. Ibid., p.45.
8. Football Task Force, *Football: Commercial Issues: a submission by the football Task Force to the Minister of Sport*. The Football Association, The FA Premier League, The Football League, *Commercial Issues: Football's Report of the Task Force* (London: Stationery Office, 1999). See also the essay by Richard Faulkner in this volume.
9. Ibid., paragraph 7.13, referring to B. Lomax, 'Supporter Representation on the Board', in *A Game of Two Halves?*, pp.200-1.
10. Ibid., paragraph 7.14.
11. See the essay by Chris Smith in this volume.
12. Supporters Direct is itself a Company Limited by Guarantee, with a broadly representative Board including David Dunn of the Co-operative Bank; Professor Eric Dunning of Leicester University; Yvonne Fletcher, Britain's first woman elected supporters' Director at Luton Town; and Peter Hunt of the Co-operative Union, as well as the three Core Group members and an independent solicitor.

4

United for Change

TREVOR BROOKING CBE

First of all I would like to say how pleased I am to be invited to make a contribution to a volume that is promoting greater supporter involvement in football clubs. I welcome the Supporters Direct initiative. The idea that supporters should be encouraged to play a responsible part in the life of the clubs they support was one of many that came from the work of the Football Task Force, of which I was a member.[1]

The Task Force succeeded in the vital task of bringing together for the first time all those concerned for the future of the game, to undertake a serious analysis of how football might best be taken forward. Although there were undoubted differences of opinion, the Task Force stimulated a lot of productive discussion on the future of football, and perhaps for the first time gave football supporters a real opportunity to have their voices heard.

Collections like this one and the conferences and publications of the Birkbeck College Football Research Unit reflect the work of the Task Force by bringing together a broad coalition of leading analysts of the game, from universities, football supporters' groups and football authorities. These conferences and publications made a major contribution to the work of the Task Force, and we are already seeing the Task Force's findings bearing fruit through the establishment of the Supporters Direct scheme.

SUPPORTERS DIRECT

Supporters Direct is vital because it addresses one of the key issues identified by the Football Task Force, namely the importance of football clubs to their local communities and the need to protect and develop this relationship. I am always struck wherever I go of how much football stimulates debate and discussion. It really is an important part of many people's lives across the country, and dear to local communities. I remember growing up in East London and going with my dad and friends to watch my local team – West Ham – play. It was a big part of the world around me. We used to watch the players on a Saturday, and go and see them afterwards. There was a local rapport and understanding.

Then of course I was lucky enough to be asked to play for the club I supported, and to come up through the youth system to play for the first team. Many of us had developed through the youth system, so we lived locally, we wandered around locally, and chatted to fans. There was a real rapport with the supporters. Even after 19 years as a player I still watch West Ham play whenever I have the chance, and still regard myself as a fan – and that to me is what football is all about. Supporters are the lifeblood of their clubs; they are a key part of the game.

So the work of the Task Force and the Birkbeck College Football Research Unit is crucial in making sure supporters remain a key part of the game. As Chair of Sport England, I believe we can all be partners in ensuring the future good health of football through initiatives like Supporters Direct. As I wrote in our 1999 *Annual Report*, Sport England is about optimizing opportunities for the whole community to take part in sport.[2] I see the Supporters Direct initiative as addressing the same agenda and I welcome it for that reason.

SPORT ENGLAND

Football, like many other sports, is a vital national asset, and our role at Sport England is to develop football and other sports throughout the country. Football can promote social interaction and inclusion so we must make sure there is continued investment in both the facilities required for people to play in, and investment in the people who keep the game alive.

Sport England is the brand name of the English Sports Council. We depend on funding from two main sources: Exchequer grant-in-aid from the Department for Culture, Media and Sport, and proceeds from the National Lottery in our role as the distributor of funds allocated to sport. Our objectives coincide with the Government's priorities of tackling social exclusion and increasing participation, and many of our programmes have these priorities at their heart.

As an organization our three main objectives are: 'More People' involved in sport, 'More Places' to play sport and 'More Medals' through higher standards of performance in sport. The key word is more – we must improve English sport. We aim to lead the development of sport in England by influencing and serving the public, private and commercial sectors, and by establishing long-term sustainable structures, which will ensure we reap results for many years to come. As part of the 'More People' programme we have assisted the football league clubs to set up academies and centres of excellence to develop the talents of local young people. Sport England and the FA Premier League are each contributing £20m over four years and clubs are also committing their own funds. The aim is to help young players achieve their footballing potential, especially those people who in the past might not have had the opportunity to play professionally. We hope that as a result more local players will break through into first teams and provide a stronger base for clubs around the country. We want to develop players who are well-rounded individuals, who are taught the importance not only of training, but also of lifestyle and diet. We want players from the local community, so that clubs will reflect the community around them, and will have a better relationship with that community. Sport England is actively encouraging this important work funded by Premier League money to help the grassroots of the game. Part of the 'More People' initiative, our own 'Active Communities' programme is also geared towards achieving greater community participation. As part of this scheme, 'Awards for All' focuses financial support on smaller groups and organizations; the 'Sports Train' initiative gets youths interested in sports and community work, and the 'School Community Sport Initiative' gives grants to schools that want to develop facilities for use not just for the school, but also by the local community.

One important scheme is at West Ham Football Club where several organizations are working together to try to increase participation of Asian people in football at all levels by providing coaching sessions and support. This is part of our overall objective to increase sporting opportunity among Asians, blacks and other ethnic communities. We have worked with the Commission for Racial Equality to appoint, jointly, two members of staff to work with the governing bodies of sport under the banner of Sporting Equals. At West Ham, along with six East London borough councils and organizations such as the Professional Footballers' Association (PFA) and Kick it Out, we hope also to bring more Asian players and supporters to the game.[3] Sport England is making an initial contribution of £35,000 a year to this scheme, encouraging Asian youngsters to play football through structured coaching programmes. The early results are very promising and some excellent young players are emerging from the scheme.

At community level Sport England has made over 400 Lottery capital building awards to football in every corner of England, ranging from a few thousand pounds for new changing rooms to several million for large leisure centres. This represents a massive investment to help provide 'More Places' for everybody who wants to play football, at whatever level. We are motivated by the need to extend opportunity for all in sport, and strongly believe that football and other sports can be a positive force for social inclusion.

A recent Lottery award of £4.5m to the Football Association Youth Trust towards a total project cost of £13.5m over three years will pay for small goals and other equipment for mini-soccer so that young boys and girls can play the game on appropriate sized facilities, as they have done in other countries for some years. (This move attracted particular support from the nine-year-old goalkeepers – the strikers may not be quite so happy about the new goals, but then they will just have to learn to shoot more accurately!)

Ultimately we hope that these initiatives will result in success and 'More Medals' for our international teams at the highest level. Strong performances in international competition excite the nation, just as poor performances invariably lead to much hand-wringing and critical self-examination. So we are supporting our top performers, in football and other sports across the country, with our 'World Class' programme designed to be a continuous support for young sportsmen and women. Sport England is working hard with its partners to promote football, particularly in the community.

The Sport England Lottery fund has been vital in improving Britain's sporting chances. By 31 March 1999 the fund had given £902.1 million to capital projects. Every community and 60 sports have benefited from Lottery funding, from clubhouses to floodlit pitches to pitch drainage. A good example of this is the Manchester Eagles Football Club. The young members of the club were devastated when vandals set fire to the trailer they used as changing rooms, but now, thanks to their own hard work and an award from the Sport England Lottery fund of £320,378, the players have a new, vandal-proof clubhouse and improved pitches. The club serves a densely populated area with a high level of crime, and it has made a real difference to the lives of young people there. There are three teams and plans to add four more, including at least one girls' team. It now functions as an FA mini-soccer centre, with 150 members. This is a real 'grass-roots' project that has helped a deprived area. The facilities are also used for mini-hockey, netball and basketball and both Manchester United's and Manchester City's 'Football in the Community' programmes include plans to play there.

UNITED FOR CHANGE

Examples like this – and others reported elsewhere in this collection – show the importance of co-operation. The various contributors to this volume represent an impressive coalition of those working together to ensure the future good health of the game, which is the aim of the Football Task Force. It is now recognized that football supporters, who have always been the lifeblood of football clubs, should have a greater involvement in the running of those clubs. This will help the professional clubs to extend and enhance their involvement in community work, and to augment the work of the many projects supported by Sport England. Ultimately, the extension of football clubs' involvement in the community will enhance the financial strength of clubs.

Now that there is a clear commitment and support from the government, supporters' groups, the PFA, the League Managers' Association, the Football Foundation and others, we can all work together to achieve this. If supporters do have a greater say in how their clubs are run, it should be to the benefit of football as a whole, both the industry and the sport.

In the past the significance of a football club to the local community has often been underestimated. Whether it is for the committed fans who travel the country to watch every game, for those who go once a year, for the people who check the results in the newspaper each week – the club has an important role to play for all these groups. It brings people together on match days and creates a sense of belonging. Quite apart from that, a local football club brings money and employment to the area. Football and all sport can make a major contribution to our society for participants and spectators alike. It is therefore quite right that the views of the people who live in that community should be taken properly into account by the football clubs they support. Football clubs need to take a far wider view than just the essential financial considerations. Of course football is a business; but it is a very special kind of business and this needs to be properly recognized and appreciated.

For this reason Sport England welcomes the new package of legal and practical support available from Supporters Direct. This is a truly constructive way for supporters to become more closely involved in their clubs. Supporters who own shares in their clubs and who can organize collectively will benefit from having a greater say in how the club is run; and board members will benefit from greater consultation with supporters' groups because no club exists without its supporters. Players too will thrive at a club that is united and well run. There is a clear opportunity here for a co-ordinated and common-sense way for supporters to become more involved. Done properly, it will be difficult for clubs not to take the reasoned debate of their supporters seriously, and over time I hope that the confidence and trust between clubs and supporters will grow.

Much has been said and written on the impact of the huge sums of money coming into the game. There is clearly a danger of supporters feeling isolated from their club and from superstar players or unknown foreign imports. Unlike my days as a fan at West Ham, now it is sometimes difficult for there to be any real rapport between a club's superstar players and their fans, so there is less of a feeling that the football club is something that comes from, and belongs to, the local community.

This is why I think the work of Sport England is so important in maintaining those links between football clubs and local communities, and nurturing a closer rapport. There has to be a role for supporters in football clubs. Football must enjoy its rude health, but it must also take its responsibilities seriously. So I welcome the debate which helps to keep the issues identified by the Football Task Force properly on the agenda. We must make sure that when decisions on the game are taken, all those concerned are sitting round the table.

Now is a very exciting time for football in this country. Many issues remain to be resolved, and I hope that we shall be able to move towards implementing more of the recommendations of the Football Task Force in the months ahead, such as the establishment of a Football Audit Commission. Ten years on from the Taylor Report the game has changed out of all recognition. With developments like Supporters Direct we are moving into a new era of increased supporter involvement in the running of football clubs and a greater accountability of clubs to their supporters and the local community. That must be the challenge. With the launch of Supporters Direct and with the broad coalition that is working together for the good of the game, it is a challenge that I am convinced can be met successfully.

NOTES

1. For details of the Task Force, see A. Brown, 'Thinking the Unthinkable or Playing the Game? Why Football Needs a Regulator', in S. Hamil, J. Michie and C. Oughton (eds.), *A Game of Two Halves? The Business of Football* (Edinburgh: Mainstream, 1999). A. Brown, 'The Football Task Force and the "Regulator Debate"', in S. Hamil, J. Michie, C. Oughton and S. Warby (eds.), *Football in the Digital Age: Whose Game Is it Anyway?* (Edinburgh: Mainstream, 2000). A. Burnham, 'The Task Force and the Future Regulation of Football', in Hamil *et al.*, *Football in the Digital Age*. N. Coward, 'Facing Football's Future: The Task Force and Beyond', in Hamil *et al.*, *Football in the Digital Age*. M. Lee, 'The Football Task Force: A Premier League View', in Hamil *et al.*, *Football in the Digital Age*. B. Lomax in this volume.
2. Sport England, *Annual Report 1998/99* (London: Sport England), p.2.
3. The Professional Footballers' Association can be contacted at 20 Oxford Court, Bishopsgate, Manchester M2 3WQ, 0161 236 0575. *Kick it Out* can be contacted at Unit 107, Business Design Centre, 52 Upper Street, London N1 0QH, tel 020 7288 6012. For details of the 'Kick it Out' campaign, see P. Power, 'Kick Racism Out of Football', in Hamil *et al.*, *Football in the Digital Age*.

5

Broadcasters v. Regulators: The Threat to Football from Media Company Ownership of Football Clubs

PETER CROWTHER

In the game between regulators and broadcasters, it is not clear who is winning. The regulators – the Office of Fair Trading, the Competition Commission and the Secretary of State for Trade and Industry – appeared to take an early lead by blocking BSkyB's attempted takeover of Manchester United, a result that had the knock-on effect of precipitating NTL's withdrawal from its bid for Newcastle United. But the broadcasters have responded by taking ownership stakes in a number of clubs: BSkyB now has stakes in five Premiership clubs, while NTL has stakes in three, and Granada a stake in one. So at present, media companies have ownership stakes in virtually half of the Premiership clubs. These recent developments raise questions about the legal grounds for intervention (if necessary) to control media ownership of football clubs. Have the media companies managed to side-step competition rules, or are there still grounds for regulation under current competition law?

The background to media ownership of football clubs in England is of course BSkyB's attempted takeover of Manchester United which was referred to the Monopolies and Mergers Commission (MMC, now the Competition Commission) for investigation and blocked by Stephen Byers, the Secretary of State for Trade and Industry, in 1999. The MMC ruled that BSkyB's ownership of Manchester United would be against the public interest because BSkyB would gain advantages which would not be open to any other broadcaster. In terms of competition in the market for broadcasting, the MMC panel concluded that ownership of Manchester United by BSkyB would reduce competition in the sale of television rights, resulting in less competition in the broadcasting industry, less innovation and less choice.[1] In addition to these arguments the MMC panel also concluded that there would be adverse effects on the organization and quality of football. These effects would arise through two channels. Firstly, if the merger went ahead, BSkyB would gain increased influence with football's regulatory authorities which could result in 'changes in the game and its presentation that might be against the public interest' as decisions would be taken in the interests of the broadcaster rather than the long-term future of the game.[2] Secondly, the panel concluded that the takeover, particularly if it precipitated other such takeovers, was likely to increase the inequality of wealth between clubs and the ability of smaller clubs to compete would be compromised.

The immediate effect of the decision to block the merger was that NTL pulled out of its proposed acquisition of Newcastle United, all of which went to show, and still shows that there is a clear public concern in relation to the ownership of football clubs by broadcasters. With its takeover of Manchester United blocked, BSkyB's response was to retain a 9.9 per cent ownership stake in Manchester United and take ownership stakes in Leeds (9.9%), Chelsea (9.9%), Sunderland (5%) and Manchester City (9.9%). At the time BSkyB purchased its stake in Manchester City the club was in the First Division but with good prospects of promotion, which was achieved at the end of the 1999/2000 season. Similarly, NTL retained a 9.8 per cent ownership stake in Newcastle United and bought further stakes in Aston Villa (9.99%) and Middlesbrough (5.5%). It is no surprise that the media companies are taking less than 10 per cent, in keeping with the Football Association's (FA) rule on dual ownership. Under this rule the FA can disregard holdings of less than 10 per cent and allow dual ownership provided that 'those shares are, in the opinion of the Council, held purely for investment purposes'.[3] However, the general assumption that the broadcasters are limiting their stakes to less than 10 per cent purely on the basis of the FA rule that prevents dual ownership of football clubs is inaccurate. Ownership stakes are also being limited partly on the basis of the current application of the merger control rules in the UK.

This essay focuses on two possible lines of intervention by the regulatory authorities that would control media ownership of football clubs. The first is the application of UK merger law, and the second concerns the case of the abuse of a dominant position through the acquisition by a dominant firm of a *not necessarily* controlling interest in a football club. The possible application of cartel law (the 'Chapter I' Prohibition contained in the Competition Act 1998) is also explored briefly.

Under UK merger laws, for the law to apply three criteria must be met. First, there must be a 'merger situation'. Second, that merger situation must 'qualify for investigation' under UK merger law; and third, the European Union (EU) merger rules must not apply – if they do, then UK law does not apply and the case would fall under the European Commission's (EC) remit.[4] It is not necessary to go into the detail of EC competition law here, rather we can take it as given that the EC merger rules would not normally apply. This is not to say that the merger would be deemed to be in the public interest or against public interest under EC competition law, only that the case would fall under UK jurisdiction and be investigated by the UK Office of Fair Trading (OFT) rather than the EC.

To return to the first question, is there a merger situation? For a merger situation to arise two enterprises have to cease to be distinct. In a general understanding of a merger, the acquisition of a 9.9 per cent stake in a football club would not amount to a merger. However, over the years the OFT has been dramatically reducing what is required in order to exercise material influence. About five years ago the general rule was that one had to acquire 25 per cent because that way one would be able to exercise material influence by, for instance, blocking any special resolution. However, over the years the authorities have broadened their view of what constitutes material influence. For example, in a 1993 case, Thomas Cook acquired 10.3 per cent of Owners Abroad and that was considered sufficient for Thomas Cook to exercise material influence. More importantly, the MMC recently looked at 'potential influence', which implies that it is no longer necessary to establish actual material influence (a legal requirement) over the conduct of the acquired company. This implies a very broad scope for the interpretation of the merger control rules regarding the existence of a merger situation. The following discussion will return to this question and illustrate it with examples from recent acquisitions. Indeed, the OFT recently found that BSkyB's acquisition of its stake in Leeds was a merger situation, until BSkyB agreed to delete its ability to have a Director appointed to the board.[5]

If it is accepted that there is a merger situation the next question is, does it qualify for investigation? To qualify for investigation a merger must satisfy one or both of two criteria. Either the assets of the acquired company must exceed £70 million or/and it must be the case that as a result of the merger the merged firm would control 25 per cent or more of the market. BSkyB's attempted acquisition of Manchester United clearly qualified for investigation because Manchester United's gross worldwide assets were in excess of £70 million. However, most football clubs do not have such assets and so it would be necessary to show that as a result of the merger 25 per cent of goods or services of a particular description would be supplied by a single entity. This is merely to establish jurisdiction and is not to be confused with the notion of the 'relevant market' (which represents an initial stage in assessing the competitive nature of the market), so the question would be whether, for instance, NTL's acquisition of 9.9 per cent of Newcastle United results in a situation where at least 25 per cent of a service of a particular kind is supplied. The OFT has not had to consider this particular question, but if, for example, the 'services of a particular kind' were top quality football in and around Newcastle, then clearly this test would be satisfied.

To take NTL as an example, NTL recently acquired 9.9 per cent through an interest free loan which is convertible in five years. Now 9.9 per cent taken on its own would probably be regarded as not sufficient to exercise material influence. However, under this deal NTL attains two further assets: the exclusive agency rights for the sale of media sponsorship and publishing, and a two-year deal covering the negotiation of television, radio and e-commerce rights. Few people will say that that does not represent an ability by NTL to materially influence the future of Newcastle's sale of its services. There is football merchandise, sponsorship, everything that is going to make the club a viable entity. So on that particular score there would appear to be a clear case to answer.

Once the jurisdictional tests have been carried out and there is a case to answer, if there is an indication that there may be some effect on competition, then that could result in a reference to the Competition Commission for investigation. This would begin a process similar to that which occurred in the BSkyB–Manchester United case. A Competition Commission panel would be convened to investigate the merger and determine whether or not it would be likely to operate against the public interest.

Moving away from the application of merger law, the second source of possible intervention is the argument that ownership stakes can constitute an abuse of a dominant position. It is important to explain the theory behind this before discussing the legal aspects. It is not necessary to acquire a controlling interest in a particular entity in order to have abused a dominant position; rather the application of the law requires first of all a dominant position, but fortunately the general consensus of the regulatory authorities is that BSkyB is dominant and therefore it seems likely that there is a case to answer.

However, there is the further question of whether this should apply only to BSkyB and not to NTL, because while NTL *may* be technically dominant in the areas within which it has an exclusive franchise for supplying cable services, the competitive situation is that wherever NTL provides cable services, it is in competition with BSkyB for the attraction of retail subscribers. So in this context the market is the market for services over which Premier League football can be supplied. This raises the question of whether NTL should be allowed to escape from the application of a rule which would otherwise apply to it but for its lack of dominance. Although this would sit comfortably with exisiting principles of competition law, it may in fact be that the broadcasters are 'collectively dominant'. Collective dominance refers to a situation where even with the existence of an allegedly single dominant company in one particular market, if the market is oligopolistic (that is, there are only a few suppliers) then it can be regarded for the purposes of competition law as collectively dominant. So in other words the allegation here would be that NTL and BSkyB are collectively abusing a dominant position for which they would then be, if that is the case and there is an abuse, jointly and separately liable. This raises the question of the nature of the abuse: the existence of a dominant position (whether collective or otherwise) is itself a 'problem' – there must be an abuse.

One approach would be to examine the impact of what has become known as the 'toehold' effect, which is the notion that possession of a part of the market gives one an advantage over those who do not have a stake in that market. Thus, if BSkyB owns Manchester United and no other broadcaster owns any other football club, then BSkyB can bid more than anyone else because some of the revenue from the next round of rights to screen live Premier League football will come back to them via their ownership of Manchester United. So if the valuation of the television rights was, say, £1 billion, BSkyB could bid in excess of that because the money comes back into the company.

Separate, but related is the notion of 'herding' which is to say that if BSkyB had bought Manchester United, other leading clubs would have a tendency to sell their rights to BSkyB. The argument is analogous to the Marks & Spencer effect – a poor analogy these days in the light of their recent performance – but the principle is that by locating your strongest attraction in the middle of the High Street, the other shops will want to locate close by.

In this context, the application of the abuse of a dominant position may rest on the argument that the abuse will take the following form. Suppose I wanted to create the Peter Crowther Football Channel. Unless I were a broadcaster in my own right and I also owned a football club I would be placed at a severe competitive disadvantage in the acquisition of television rights when bidding against other broadcasters who owned clubs. In other words, the market is effectively narrowed down to the broadcasters (channel providers are not necessarily broadcasters). This brings us on to a further issue which is the application of cartels. If NTL and BSkyB own stakes in almost half of the Premier League clubs, this raises the prospect – at least in principle – of tacit (or explicit) collusion. This matter is not considered further here, for lack of evidence.

If the investments in football clubs are not caught by the merger rules, it is unlikely that they would be treated as anti-competitive agreements in the absence of very persuasive evidence. Under recent UK legislation, UK competition law generally will not apply to 'vertical' agreements, that is, an agreement between a broadcaster and a football club. So in order to demonstrate that there is an *anti-competitive* agreement, it must be shown that there is an abusively dominant position within the meaning of the UK law, or it must be shown that there is an anti-competitive agreement under EC law. This raises the question of the possible effect on trade between member states, but in terms of the sale of the broadcasting rights, it may be possible to show that there is a potential effect on trade between member states.

A second question which may arise is, how can it be shown that one single agreement is anti-competitive? Under competition law this problem may be overcome where there is what is called a 'network of similar effects', which is to say that even if it cannot be shown that the acquisition by NTL of 9.9 per cent in Newcastle is anti-competitive *per se*, if there are a whole range of similar agreements, the net effect can be to have an anti-competitive market situation and that will fall under the competition rules. This would be the case both under the EC and UK rules.

To summarize, there are good reasons to expect media control of football clubs to operate against the public interest. There is also a legal basis for intervention and certainly from my understanding the OFT is already taking an interest in this situation as is (separately) the European Commission. But it will require a broad-minded approach to the application of competition rules because competition law typically takes a very lenient view of vertical agreements.

However, the nature of the football industry – and the approach taken by the MMC – shows that this is one area within which there should be a very strong exception to the otherwise very sensible rule.

NOTES

1. N. Finney, 'The MMC's Inquiry into BSkyB's Merger with Manchester United plc', in S. Hamil, J. Michie, C. Oughton and S. Warby (eds.), *Football in the Digital Age: Whose Game Is it Anyway?* (Edinburgh: Mainstream, 2000), pp.77–8.
2. Ibid., p.79.
3. A. Brown, 'Sneaking in Through the Back Door? Media Company Interests and Dual Ownership of Football Clubs', in Hamil *et al.*, *Football in the Digital Age*, p.89.
4. There is an exception to this rule, under which a national competition authority may request that a case be 'handed back'.
5. OFT press release, August 2000.

6

The Legacy of the Football Task Force

RICHARD FAULKNER

As the Vice Chair of the Football Task Force I am very pleased to have the opportunity to contribute to this volume on supporters' involvement in football clubs and the whole Supporters Direct initiative. Involving supporters was one of the main points addressed in the final Football Task Force report on commercial issues in football.[1] This was delivered in December 1999 and I am pleased that this collection contains essays by so many people who contributed to the Task Force process in so many different ways.

The specific issue of Supporters Direct is dealt with in some detail by other contributors to this volume, so I intend to concentrate on describing the context from which Supporters Direct emerged; the work of the Football Task Force, and in particular its final *Commercial Issues* report.[2]

THE TASK FORCE MEMBERSHIP

Looking back, it is clear that there was one fundamental mistake made when the Task Force was established in July 1997. It was not, in retrospect, sensible to select the members of the Task Force effectively as delegates from nominated organizations, because in that the seeds of eventual conflict were being sown. The diametrically opposed interests represented were unlikely to be able to come together to agree a unanimous report on commercial issues.

The Chairman and I sought to tackle this in a number of different ways. In the first year and a half of the Task Force's work, we appointed a core working group, some of whom were independent members; and some of these 'independents' were also then added to the main Task Force. So by the end the Task Force contained a mixture of three groups: representatives of the football authorities, representatives of the supporters' associations, and a number of independents. If I were starting the Task Force again I would only appoint independent individuals who would be chosen for their knowledge, their reputation and good sense. It would then be their job to receive representations from the football authorities and the supporters' organizations, and these independent members would then be expected to make up their minds objectively. Had the Task Force membership been composed entirely of independent members, we would still have produced a report that closely resembled the version that has now become known as the 'majority report'[3]. It was through the support of the independents on the Task Force that the majority report carried the day.

THE TASK FORCE'S TERMS OF REFERENCE

The Task Force's terms of reference were to examine how:

1. racism might be eliminated from football and how to encourage wider participation by ethnic minorities, both in playing and spectating.
2. to improve disabled access to spectating facilities.
3. to encourage greater supporter involvement in the running of clubs.
4. to encourage ticketing and pricing policies geared to reflect the needs of all on an equitable basis, including for cup and international matches.
5. to encourage merchandising policies reflecting the needs of supporters as well as commercial considerations.
6. to develop the opportunities for players to act as good role models in terms of behaviour and sportsmanship and actively to become involved in community schemes.
7. to reconcile the potential conflict between the legitimate needs of shareholders, players and supporters where clubs are floated on the Stock Exchange.

The Task Force should be judged against whether or not it complied with those terms of reference.

My own view is that it did, and more effectively and with a greater degree of consensus than seemed likely at the beginning. David Mellor was an excellent Chairman and I agree with Ian Todd, the Chairman of the National Federation of Football Supporters Clubs, when he says that 'whatever view you hold of Mellor as a former MP and radio presenter or in relation to his other activities, he proved a very capable Chairman of the Task Force, his legal training being of great benefit in drawing out opinions and ensuring statements were backed up by reason'.

We addressed the issue of racism in the first report, disabled access in the second, and community involvement in the third.[4] Supporter involvement in the running of clubs was touched upon in the third report but looked at in more detail in the fourth report on *Commercial Issues*[5] along with ticketing prices, merchandising and reconciling the conflict between supporters and shareholders.

The consultative process we went through, which involved many supporters' groups, and led to the drafting of each report, was very extensive and very thorough. The central element in it was the programme of away days to the major cities of England, during which we took evidence during the day and held well-attended public open meetings in the evenings. Those who made the greatest contribution to these away day events were Eleanor Oldroyd of BBC Radio 5, who chaired every public meeting brilliantly, and Graham Kelly, the former Chief Executive of the Football Association (FA). Graham attended virtually every public meeting and withstood fans' battery of criticism of the FA with remarkable good humour. What impressed all of us about these occasions was the strength of feeling displayed by the supporters which at times approached outrage over the way they felt they were being treated by those who control and in many cases own their game.

THE TASK FORCE'S RECOMMENDATIONS ON ISSUES OF RACISM AND DISABILITY

We were very impressed by the fans' concerns on the social issues, and the universal repugnance for racism within football and total support for the 'Kick It Out' campaign. Everywhere we went we found sympathy and a genuine willingness to do something about the problems of people with disabilities in getting access to and enjoying facilities in football grounds. We were able to produce unanimous reports (with recommendations for action) from the Task Force on both the issues of racism and disability.[6] The Task Force made one specific policy recommendation to the government on racism, which was that a new offence should be created of racist chanting. This was accepted and passed into law via a private members bill in the course of 1999.

COMMUNITY INVOLVEMENT BY FOOTBALL CLUBS

The third Task Force report addressed the issue of players as role models, and recommended that clubs enforce contracts which provide for their players to work in the community for a specified number of hours each week.[7] This was supported by all the members of the Task Force except for, sadly, the representative of the Professional Footballers' Association (PFA). The rest of the Task Force members took the view that if the contracts of players earning £10,000 a week and upwards contained a provision that a couple of hours each week should be spent with underprivileged children or in an old people's home or in a hospital, then clubs should enforce that. The Chief Executive of a major Premier League club who said 'Yes, it's in the contract but we can't get the Manager to take it seriously' did not impress us. On this issue we lost the PFA representative from the Task Force.

Our recommendation in that same third report on the community, that the Premier League allocate a fixed proportion of its income from the next television broadcasting deal for distribution throughout the grassroots of the game was accepted, and we look forward to that coming on stream soon.[8] And so too was the groundbreaking proposal that funding be made available to back the establishment of supporters' trusts and thus herald the establishment of a real consumer voice in football decision taking. This initiative has now taken physical shape with the provision of funds by the Department of Culture, Media and Sport to enable the establishment of Supporters Direct.

THE *COMMERCIAL ISSUES* REPORT: THE EVIDENCE

The third Task Force report, *Investing in the Community*, was published in January 1999.[9] Work then commenced on the final, and most difficult of all the reports, that concerning commercial issues in football. This final report went to the heart of the Task Force's terms of reference. How it responded to these issues would determine how the whole Task Force process would be judged. If the Task Force had ducked its responsibilities and failed to meet the aspirations of both the Government and the football supporters, it would have been derided and criticized and the Task Force process would have ended in dishonour. But equally there was no point in producing a report that was so radical but unrealistic that Kate Hoey, the Minister for Sport, could not take it seriously or have it approved by her colleagues. Nevertheless, the Task Force did have to take as its starting point the assumption that there were things seriously wrong with the game and with its governance. That this assumption was fully justified became clear as the depth of dissatisfaction expressed by football's 'consumers', the supporters, unfolded at every one of our public meetings. The validity of this operating assumption was also supported by the results of detailed research from the Sir Norman Chester Centre for Football Research at Leicester University, commissioned in conjunction with the Premier League, the Football League and the FA.[10] The Task Force felt it needed to commission this to rebut any claims that the public meetings were attended by an unrepresentative sample of football supporters, and to give greater depth to the impressions gained at those meetings.

Much valuable information was also acquired from work previously undertaken by one of the Task Force members, Sir John Smith.[11] Sir John carried out an inquiry on behalf of the FA into financial impropriety in the game in response to the so-called 'bung' scandal regarding illegal 'under-the-counter' payments to players' agents to facilitate transfers. In his report Sir John states that supporter loyalty for his or her team lasts 'from the cradle to the grave'. This makes football a very unusual consumer product with the relationship between producer and consumer unlike that in any other industry. The attachment that individual churchgoers have to their church is perhaps a comparable relationship. But then you are not charged for your seat at a religious service and you do not often find worshippers buying replica cassocks from a church shop with the vicar's name on the back!

The football product may be on offer in scores of outlets every day of the week. So in theory the consumer is free to choose which supplier's product he or she prefers. But in practice each club is a monopoly supplier. A conventional economic framework of analysis might suggest that the Newcastle United supporters who took legal action against their club's board of directors because they were being compelled to move seats (the 'Save our Seats' campaign) should respond by taking their custom down the road to Sunderland, Hartlepool or Darlington. But of course in reality this does not happen as each club's fans are compelled by emotional power to enter into and actively maintain a monopoly supplier relationship with their club.

So what were the issues which the Task Force research indicated supporters felt most strongly about? Of overwhelming importance was ticket prices; 60 per cent said they were not happy with the level of prices and half said the clubs had not got their pricing right.[12] And no wonder! The Task Force compared prices before the Hillsborough disaster with 1999 prices; the average price of an adult non-concessionary ticket in 1988 and 1989 was £4.03, but by 1999 it was £17.42, a price increase of 331 per cent. The rate of increase for season tickets was much the same over the same period. Overall price inflation in the economy, as measured by the retail price index (RPI), rose by 54.8 per cent over the same period. Given these figures it is therefore hardly surprising that 70 per cent of those who have stopped going to matches or who hardly ever go say that ticket price increases are the main reason for their non-attendance.

There was a range of other consumer issues which we encountered, including poor and discriminatory treatment of away fans, inconsistency in practices regarding the supply of concessionary tickets across clubs (and sometimes their complete unavailability) and consumer exploitation in the marketing of replica kits. All of these are detailed in the *Commercial Issues* report.[13]

The Task Force also examined the issue of the involvement of supporters in the running of the game. It gathered a lot of evidence on the effects of stock market flotation and found that three-quarters of supporters believed that flotation was a recipe for conflict between their interests and those of shareholders. Forty-nine per cent said that flotation made it harder for fans to feel closer to their clubs and to have a say in their future. The Task Force also received some allegations of horrifying financial impropriety and examples of how club grounds had been sold for private gain.

The Task Force was thorough in its evidence gathering. And as so much of what was discovered could not be ignored, given the depth of supporter disquiet uncovered regarding recent developments in the game, it was obvious that the Task Force would have to produce some radical proposals to deal with these problems.

THE *COMMERCIAL ISSUES* REPORT RECOMMENDATIONS

There was overwhelming support in the Task Force for some form of independent regulation and a means of providing a consumer voice for disaffected fans. But the challenge was to present a realistic proposal to address this demand while retaining the unity of all the Task Force members.

For a while this looked as though it might be possible. In August 1999 the football authorities (the FA, the Premier League, and the Football League) produced a paper that contained several significant proposals. These included: (1) the setting up of an independent scrutiny panel (ISP) performing a function not unlike that of the British Standards Institution (BSI) or the Audit Commission; (2) the carrying out of a 'health check' audit on the state of regulation, best practice and governance in the game on a regular basis; and (3) the establishment of best practice guidelines. Most of us on the Task Force took the view that this represented a huge step forward. It was very much in line with the new approach that the FA's new chairman Geoff Thompson was already bringing to the Football Association, where he was promoting major changes in corporate governance. This included action to implement Sir John Smith's recommendations for dealing with financial impropriety, as the FA established a compliance unit to deal with financial irregularities led by former Football Supporters Association chairman Graham Bean.

The independent members of the Task Force at least would have signed up to a report which gave the FA, as the game's governing body, a clearly defined role as a regulation enforcer. Accordingly we produced a further draft of the *Commercial Issues* report which made the football authorities' proposal for an independent scrutiny panel the centrepiece of the new regulatory framework. Most supporters' groups would have accepted this approach, at least on a two-year trial basis, provided that the independent scrutiny panel was genuinely independent and was a permanent standing body.

Unfortunately the football authorities eventually decided that they could not live with this and as a consequence it was agreed that they should produce their own report[14] and that the other members of the Task Force would submit theirs.[15] Both would be published and presented to the Minister for Sport, Kate Hoey MP, and she would be responsible for deciding which offered the most effective way forward.

The football authorities' final paper (the minority report) represents a step forward compared with their position three years previously.[16] This alone justifies a large part of the Task Force process. They did, for example, accept the need for a customer charter and a code of best practice; they proposed some valuable safeguards to prevent the sale of grounds without a proper consultation process and the securing of a new long-term home, exactly what would have prevented the scandal at Brighton. They stuck with their plans for an Independent Scrutiny Panel which would review and assess the quality of the system of regulation, best practice and governance provided by the football authorities.

So there was much common ground with the findings recommended by the representatives of the supporters' groups and the independents in the majority report.

However, the Task Force members who did not represent the various football authorities felt that more radical action was required. Hence the central recommendation in the majority report that a Football Audit Commission (FAC) should be established whose members would be appointed by the Secretary of State for Culture, Media and Sport and which would be wholly independent of the football authorities. In addition, the creation of an 'Ombudsfan' was proposed who would adjudicate on the grievances of ordinary supporters, and refer cases to the FAC when necessary.

The majority report also envisaged that the FAC would be a permanent body, wholly independent of the game's authorities. It would be able to investigate clubs and enforce sanctions in the case of exploitative merchandising. For example, clubs would not be able to change their kits for at least two seasons, to prevent fans from having frequently to buy replica shirts. The proposed FAC would also enforce a 'stretching' policy on ticket prices so that those at the top end of the price range would subsidize those at the bottom.

The majority report also recommended the setting up of a Football Compliance Unit to police financial irregularities, subject to review by the FAC. A constitutionally entrenched code of practice setting out minimum standards of conduct by clubs was also recommended; to be drafted by the FAC in consultation with the football authorities, clubs and supporters.

In addition, the sale of any ground would have to be approved by the FAC, as a protection against asset-stripping.

The majority report was particularly enthusiastic about the potential for supporter-shareholder trusts in promoting the interests of supporters citing with approval a similar conclusion in Sir Norman Chester's famous 1968 *Report of the Committee of Football* for the Department of Education and Science.[17] The explosion in the number of independent supporters associations and the experience of supporter-shareholder trusts at Northampton Town FC and AFC Bournemouth were evidence of the beneficial effects of greater fan involvement in the ownership and administration of clubs. The majority report specifically recommended that where a club wished to float on the stock market, it should have an obligation to satisfy the FAC that this was in the best interests of the club and supporters. Any club that floated on the stock market would first have to make 25 per cent of all shares available to season ticket holders. Amongst other recommendations were calls that all clubs recognize and encourage as a collective body supporter trusts and supporter-shareholder associations; this could involve promoting a representative from a supporter group on to the club board in a director or observer capacity.[18] Similarly, it recommended that the FAC should investigate means of encouraging the collectivization of supporters' shareholdings; this should include advising supporter-shareholders, including current shareholders, how to hold their shares in a collective or mutual trust form.[19]

THE PUBLICATION OF THE TASK FORCE *COMMERCIAL ISSUES* REPORT
AND AFTERMATH

These were a set of recommendations with real force. It was then a matter for government to take the proposals forward. There was much detailed material in the final *Commercial Issues* report on how it was intended that a code of practice should be enforced, how standards should be set and above all how sanctions should be applied by the Football Audit Commission. These proposals were intended to make a real difference if clubs treated their fans badly. If fans had reason for complaint at any club the Task Force recommended that there should be established machinery for those complaints to be considered independently and officially. If that showed that somebody had done wrong, then there would be a provision for sanctions and for fines. These were significant recommendations, which if implemented would make a huge difference.

We did not take any vote inside the Task Force and put people on the spot and say which version they wished to support. However, both the Chairman and I made clear at the launch on 23 December 1999 that we preferred the more radical majority document, and so did virtually all the independent members of the Task Force. This was backed by a letter from 11 members of the Task Force to the Minister for Sport on 27 January 2000 urging implementation of the majority recommendations. That letter was signed by all the representatives of the supporters' associations and virtually all the independents, including David Mellor and myself. The majority report also had the unanimous support of the All Party Football Committee in the House of Commons. An early day motion (EDM) was tabled in January 2000 congratulating supporters on their constructive work in the deliberations of the Football Task Force. The EDM further welcomed the majority report, supported its recommendations for greater supporter involvement and called for a strong code of practice with the appointment of a Football Audit Commission to provide independent regulation. The motion also supported the appointment of an 'Ombudsfan' to act as the consumer's champion. It also accepted that the football authorities had made some progress in addressing the serious problem of financial impropriety, but expressed regrets that the proposals contained in the minority report fell short of what was required. It called upon the Government and the FA to implement majority report without delay.

It would be wrong to overlook the initiatives made by the football authorities. Their earlier recommendations made substantial progress in terms of creating a more tolerant attitude towards accommodating spectators with disabilities in grounds, and in combating racism in football.

Overall the Task Force has made a difference. Although it did not get everything it wanted and it has not delivered everything everyone asked for, at the end of the process things are better than they were at the beginning. From that point of view the Football Task Force process has been worthwhile.

NOTES

1. Football Task Force, *Football: Commercial Issues* (London: Stationery Office, 1999). The Football Association, The FA Premier League, The Football League, *Commercial Issues: Football's Report to the Football Task Force* (London: Stationery Office, 1999).
2. Ibid.
3. Football Task Force, *Football: Commercial Issues.*
4. Football Task Force, *Eliminating Racism from Football.* (London: Stationery Office 1998). Football Task Force, *Improving Facilities for Disabled Supporters.* (London: Stationery Office, 1998). Football Task Force, *Investing in the Community* (London: Stationery Office, 1999).
5. Football Task Force, *Football: Commercial Issues.* The Football Association *et al.*, *Commercial Issues: Football's Report to the Football Task Force.*
6. Football Task Force, *Eliminating Racism from Football.* Football Task Force, *Improving Facilities for Disabled Supporters.*
7. Football Task Force, *Investing in the Community.*
8. Ibid.
9. Ibid.
10. J. Williams, and S. Perkins, *Ticket Pricing, Football Business, and 'Excluded' Football Fans: Research on the "new economics" of football match attendance in England* (University of Leicester: Sir Norman Chester Centre for Football Research, 1998) in Football Task Force, *Football: Commercial Issues*, Appendix C (London: Stationery Office. 1999).
11. Sir John Smith and M. LeJeune, *Football: Its values, Finances and Reputation* (London: The Football Association, 1998).
12. Williams and Perkins, *Ticket Pricing, Football Business, and 'Excluded' Football Fans.*
13. Football Task Force, *Football: Commercial Issues.*
14. The Football Association *et al.*, *Commercial Issues: Football's Report to the Football Task Force.*
15. Football Task Force, *Football: Commercial Issues.*
16. The Football Association *et al.*, *Commercial Issues: Football's Report to the Football Task Force.*
17. Football Task Force, *Football: Commercial Issues*, pp.29–33, 34–40. Sir Norman Chester, *Report on the Committee on Football* (London: Department of Education and Science, 1968).
18. Football Task Force, *Football: Commercial Issues*, p.33.
19. Ibid., p.40.

7

Time for Change: Supporters Direct

ANDY BURNHAM

I have always believed that football clubs belong more to their supporters than their shareholders. Some people may have bits of paper to say they own a club's assets – stadium, training ground, brand – but the heart and soul of every club is the property of its fans. Yet for all the financial and emotional investment we make in our football clubs, the return we get back in terms of genuine say and influence is negligible. When we think of how sport is run, there is a perception that football is at the forefront of best practice and change. But if our yardstick is how much a club involves and consults its supporters, other sports come out better.

In the 1980s my family were season ticket holders at Everton and Lancashire CCC. Those were the days – and how long ago they seem now – when we would get an annual summons to Goodison to have our family photograph taken with the spoils of the preceding campaign. It was always a great day – but match days apart it was about as far as our involvement with the club went. Being a 'member' of Lancashire meant something more. Membership was open to anyone and for the reasonable cost of a season ticket you got an equal voice with the other members in the affairs of the club. For many years, my father went to the AGM to vote in favour of women being given access to the main pavilion. It was narrowly defeated on a number of occasions – 'there'll be pushchairs, toys and everything lying around if we let them in' – but the democratic nature of the process could not be faulted and eventually the argument was won.

County cricket clubs are clubs in the traditional sense – a collective and inclusive society that belongs first and foremost to its members. That is their strength. Whereas individuals will always make mistakes and errors of judgement, there is a better chance that a group of people who have the best interests of an organization at heart will collectively come to the right decision about its future. Many European football clubs are true to this model – and Barcelona is of course the prime example – but football clubs in this country have always operated along different lines. It is more of a take-it-or-leave-it approach with the underlying assumption being that football supporters can be expected to turn up week in week out regardless of how they are treated.

The flawed nature of the relationship between football clubs and their supporters was brought home to me over the year that I worked for the Football Task Force. One of the points in the Government's remit to the Task Force was to 'encourage greater supporter involvement in the running of clubs'. The most striking thing about working on the Task Force was just how common it was for boards and fans to be in open conflict. Board members would come and talk about fans' groups as if they were the enemy and vice versa.

This mutual distrust between board and fans was repeated at clubs across the country and followed the same debilitating pattern. Bad feeling aired daily in the local press would lead to low morale, low gates, unstable finances and, eventually, poor performance in the league. Once a club was on this downward spiral, it would be hard to break out of it. And the more entrenched the two sides, the deeper the problems on and off the pitch became.

One striking example came from an official supporters' club which only a few years earlier had organized fundraising buckets on street corners to save the club after it had fallen into administration. They had poured hundreds of thousands of pounds in to the ailing club's coffers and, as their sole aim was the club's survival, had asked for nothing in return for their investment. A few years later – with the club back in good health – the fans told us how the club's new management were trying to evict them from the supporters' club so that it could be turned into an executive suite.

It was clear to me that a game as great as this must be able to come up with a better way of doing things. Surely it must be possible to run a club that values and involves fans? And – crucially – would that not help the commercial side of the club's activities? The answer in both cases is yes but – with a few honourable exceptions – the world of football has not yet caught on.

Brian Lomax was one of the architects of the Northampton Town Supporters' Trust. It was formed out of emergency meetings when the club had fallen into administration. The Northampton fans did not just want to pour money into the club and prop up a regime which they believed had got them into such dire straits in the first place. They wanted a proper say in the future of the club in return for their financial support. Their decision has paid rich dividends. The prize has not just been healthier gates and a better league position, though that would be enough. The involvement of the supporters' trust in the club's affairs has brought improvements in so many other areas: first-class facilities for disabled people, an effective anti-racism policy and energetic football in the community scheme.

These things seemed to me to be worth striving for. A well-run football club has the potential to give so much back to its local community. But what makes the case for a more inclusive model of running a club so compelling and complete is that it also makes commercial sense. Brian once explained how Northampton Town had put a series of options on ticket price increases to the vote amongst members of the supporters trusts (a £3 raise equals £500,000 transfer kitty and so on). Members of the trust voted unanimously for the biggest price increase.

Supporters will willingly part with their money to support the club when they feel consulted and involved. What we do not like is being taken for granted – and expected to pay for massive percentage increases without any explanation as to why they are needed. The more positive people feel about their club, the more likely it is that they will buy that plastic sun visor with the club crest that they have always wanted. For all the business expertise that football has imported over the last few years, it still surprises me how few clubs have really grasped this point.

So in the Football Task Force report *Investing in the Community* we proposed that a mechanism be established to help supporters at other clubs develop trusts similar to that at Northampton.[1] In short, making clubs more like clubs again. Last year, the Government accepted this recommendation and since then a lot of work has gone in to developing the Supporters Direct scheme. It will be fully functional for the start of the 2000/2001 season.

There are two standard arguments deployed against the idea of supporters' ownership of clubs. The first – that the ways of the boardroom are beyond the understanding of supporters and that they cannot be trusted to respect the confidentiality of club affairs – can be easily dismissed. In relation to the former argument, in 1997 Peter Johnson, then chairman of Everton FC, engaged in what many supporters regarded as a grossly inadequate piece of business planning with regard to the proposed move of Everton's ground from its inner-city Liverpool site at Goodison Park to an out-of-town site. A group of supporters, appalled at the lack of rigour with which the various options were drawn up, proceeded to organize the 'Goodison for Everton' campaign which lobbied for a more coherent and thoughtful approach to the consideration of options. The reasonable force and professionalism of their arguments were in sharp relief to the antics of the club management.[2] On the question of confidentiality, supporter directors are already proving the critics wrong and showing that they can be trusted to work in a responsible way. But confidentiality is not always in a club's best interests. It was Brighton and Doncaster fans who spoke out and blew the whistle on wrongdoing at their clubs, not their boards of directors. Famously, at Doncaster the chairman was actually conspiring to burn the main stand.

The second is that talk of supporters owning clubs is fanciful and pie-in-the-sky. This is harder to knock down. If owning a big club outright is your goal, then of course it is a difficult challenge. But if your goal is simply to secure a small part of the club – and thereby a more influential voice in its affairs – that is achievable. The smaller the club you support, the better your chances of success. It just takes enough people to believe that change is possible.

Supporters' trusts are part of the answer to the debate about whether there should be a statutory regulator for football. We all want more Northamptons and no more Doncasters. But is a statutory regulator really the best way of achieving that goal? I do not believe that there are many fans in the country who would welcome the prospect of an independent regulator telling their club what price it could or could not charge for tickets. While many people support the abstract principle of lower ticket prices, they hold fast to the autonomy of their own club. I am in no doubt that the best way of achieving the better running of football clubs is the proper involvement of fans at every level.

How will we know if Supporters Direct has been a success? If it helps just a handful of clubs forge a better relationship with their fans – and as a result achieve a sounder financial footing – then it will have been worthwhile. This is already happening. A trust has been established at Luton Town and a supporters' representative elected to the board. But I am hopeful that it will achieve much more. I believe that it will help change opinions within the game about the positive role that football supporters have to play in the running of the game. The turning point will come when it becomes known that clubs with a better relationship with their supporters sell more season tickets. And there is nothing wrong with that.

NOTES

1. Football Task Force, *Investing in the Community* (London: Stationery Office, 1999).
2. For further discussion on the management practices at Everton FC under its former chairman Peter Johnson see T. Cannon and S. Hamil, 'Reforming Football's Boardrooms', in S. Hamil, J. Michie, C. Oughton and S. Warby (eds.), *Football in the Digital Age: Whose Game Is it Anyway?* (Edinburgh: Mainstream, 2000).

PART 2
Supporters' Trusts in Action

8

Mutualism Rules: The Community in Football

KEVIN JAQUISS

In Spring 2000, on a cold grey day in South London, a new form of financial instrument was launched by the Crystal Palace Supporters' Trust. It promised no rate of interest, no financial return, and no right to repayment of capital. In fact, the proper assumption as an investor was that you would never see your money again.

The people who launched the Loan Capital Fund did it because their football club was in trouble and they thought that other supporters would put their hands in their pockets to keep it alive. In the end 4,000 people joined the supporters' trust and the Loan Capital Fund raised over £1 million, all in about two months.

In the words of Sir Alex Ferguson after the 1999 European Cup Final – 'Football, eh? Bloody hell'.

WHAT'S SPECIAL ABOUT FOOTBALL CLUBS?

In an essay entitled 'Football, Fans and Fat Cats: Whose Football Club Is it Anyway?' I discuss the special relationship between supporters and their club.[1] That relationship might be reflected in a legal structure based on modern ideas about mutualism. The final section of the piece is headed 'Pie in the Sky?'. The experience at Crystal Palace and at other clubs in England and Scotland (including clubs in the Premier League) shows that it is not.

Anyone who supports a football club knows what the people at Crystal Palace meant when they used the slogan 'Save our Club'. They did not own the club in any way the law would recognize, but it was 'theirs' and they probably felt more strongly about it than some of the people who actually owned it in the past. They and their community would have suffered had the club ceased to exist. That is why they were prepared to contribute such huge sums of money to a loan fund which was unlikely to pay them back. They did not want to own the club financially, to make money from it. They just wanted the club to continue to play its part in their community.

But it went deeper than that. Underlying the love of the club and the anxiety for its future was a deep frustration, a sense that those who managed the club had let the supporters down. They did not want to pour money into the club only to see it squandered by a new management. They wanted a say in how the club was managed, to try to make sure that the same thing would not happen again and to cement the club into its proper place in the community.

At the time of writing it has just been announced that Simon Jordan is to buy Crystal Palace, and the future of the club seems secure. The £1 million in the Loan Capital Fund is no longer needed to save the club but the supporters' trust has issued a press release welcoming the takeover (and stressing its role in bringing Mr Jordan to the negotiating table). Mr Jordan has said that he will discuss with the Trust the possibility of it buying a stake in the club and having an elected representative on the Board. The end result may be a supporters' trust which is truly representative of fans, operates in a democratic way and has a real say in the life of the club.

If so, both the club and the community will benefit. The conflict which exists between some clubs and their supporters (over ticket policies and replica kit prices, to give two examples) is bad for football but it is also bad business. A club which builds bridges with the community it serves is always more likely to thrive than one which is perceived as treating its supporters with contempt.

SUPPORTERS DIRECT

The aim of Supporters Direct is to help 'people who want to play a responsible part in the life of the club they support'. In practice, this means that the people concerned will have to be organized and to speak with one voice. Supporters Direct has recognized that this will involve groups getting advice about legal structures and has set up a means for them to do so cheaply and efficiently. A structure is necessary to ensure that supporters, and clubs who deal with them, know exactly where they stand.

Some critics of the Supporters Direct initiative have pointed to the danger that supporters' groups could be used as a platform for self-promotion by their leading members and that, in extreme cases, a group of supporters could turn into just another bunch of greedy investors in football.

For that reason, Supporters Direct has made it clear in its promotional literature that it will only support groups which are 'based on democratic, mutual and not for profit principles'. By making sure that the groups it helps have the right type of constitution, Supporters Direct can have confidence that it will operate in the interests of supporters, their club and the community.

DEMOCRATIC, MUTUAL AND NOT-FOR-PROFIT STRUCTURES

Each of these three elements (democracy, mutualism and not for profit) is important and can be delivered through a number of different legal structures. Supporters Direct will be promoting companies limited by guarantee, industrial and provident societies and trusts. The industrial and provident society model is particularly appropriate where a supporters' group needs to raise money by issuing some form of circular (as happened at Crystal Palace). This is because special rules apply to the issuing of a circular by certain types of industrial and provident society. There are, however, some other advantages in the model despite its unfamiliarity and it will therefore be used as an illustration of the way a legal structure can be made to match what supporters' groups need.

The Co-operative Party, Birkbeck College and Cobbetts have worked together to produce a set of Model Rules for a 'football community mutual' and it is appropriate to look at the way the three Supporters Direct principles of democracy, mutualism and not for profit are dealt with in the model.

DEMOCRACY

Every member of a football community mutual has one share and one vote. You do not get more votes by putting in more money or talking louder than anyone else. Your liability for what the mutual does is limited to the cost of the share (usually £1).

The mutual is run by a non-executive Board of directors drawn from the community served by the football club. At least half of the directors will be elected by the members and the others will be co-opted by the Board under an open Board Membership Policy designed to ensure that the Society Board has the skills and experience which it needs to operate effectively and that the interests of the community are adequately represented. This means that representatives of groups like the local authority, the young, local business, employees of the club, the Sports Council or Football in the Community might be appointed.

As well as electing the majority of the Board, members of the mutual will attend general meetings to hear reports and approve budgets and policy statements. Most supporters' groups are also eager to use the Internet to communicate and many intend to use postal ballots for elections and major decisions to ensure that the results are as representative as possible.

It is possible to build creatively on this basic structure where there is a special need. In the case of Crystal Palace, the plan was to raise very large sums of money and the intention was to work in large units for donations. In the end, the minimum donation to the Loan Capital Fund was £1,000. This created the potential difficulty that even fanatical supporters of Crystal Palace might have trouble in persuading their wives and husbands to hand their family savings to the mutual to be spent at the whim of the membership. The answer was to give the contributors to the Fund the right to vote between them on any proposal to buy shares which the mutual negotiated and the right to elect some members of the mutual Board. Voting within the Loan Capital Fund was slightly weighted in favour of those who had contributed larger sums of money.

MUTUALISM

Many of the structures which have come out of the 'new mutualism' movement in recent years do not fit the classic definition of a mutual which was developed in Victorian England. Under that definition, people joined together to own a business which was delivering a service to them – in order to be a customer you had to be an owner and in order to be an owner you had to be a customer.

A football community mutual is not there simply to serve the economic interests of its members but it is a mutual in the contemporary sense. The key relationship is between the mutual and the community it serves. The community is served by the mutual and owns it (through open membership) and controls it (through the elected and co-opted members of the Board).

A football community mutual stands in the great tradition of people doing things for themselves when they were not getting what they wanted. A key aspect of this is that different people bring different skills. Many supporters' groups have talent at their disposal which matches or surpasses in some areas the talent on the Board of their club.

NOT FOR PROFIT

The rules of a football community mutual require its business to be conducted for the benefit of the community and not for the profit of its members. The profits are not to be distributed in any way whatsoever among the members and the shares carry no right to any interest, dividend or bonus. If the mutual is wound up, any surplus after the debts are paid has to go to charity or to another industrial and provident society run for the benefit of the community. All of this means that a football mutual cannot be used as a vehicle for making profit and that its assets (which could include shares in a football club) cannot be cashed in by unscrupulous members in the future.

A very important feature of the model is that an industrial and provident society registered to conduct its business for the benefit of the community *cannot* benefit its members. The Registry of Friendly Societies, with which the football community mutual is registered, will not register any change in rules which would permit this to happen. There are statutory provisions under which an industrial and provident society can convert to a company (making it easier for changes to the constitution to be made) but it is possible to provide real safeguards against this happening except on the clearest possible wish of the total membership.

All of this makes fairly clear what a football community mutual is *not* about. But it is important to be clear what we mean when we talk about a football community mutual benefiting the community. The model rules set out two key aims:

- to strengthen the bonds between the football club and the community which it serves and to represent the interests of the community in the running of the football club.

- to benefit present and future members of the community served by the football club by promoting, encouraging and furthering the game of football as a recreational facility, sporting activity and focus for community involvement.

These aims reflect the aspirations of groups of supporters at most of the professional football clubs in England and are the basis upon which the mutual is registered with the Registry of Friendly Societies. They are therefore a key constitutional commitment. The Registry would not register any change to them unless the change could be shown to continue to deliver a benefit to the community and not to the members of the mutual.

None of this means that a football community mutual cannot make a profit; it simply means that any profit would have to be used for the benefit of the community. A mutual which ended up owning a football club would take on paid executives and entrust them with the efficient and profitable running of the club. The modern industrial and provident society model lends itself to this. There can be a clear distinction between the role of the Board – who are there to represent the community's interests and supervise the running of the club – and the executive – who are there as professional managers to run the club. It might be argued that some of the problems in football clubs run as companies have been caused by a lack of clarity about who does what and that the mutual structure brings a real benefit here.

WHAT HAPPENS NEXT?

Supporters' groups, based on the principles of democracy, mutualism and not for profit, are springing up all over the country and the level of enquiries to Supporters Direct suggests that there will eventually be a group at most clubs. This gives rise to questions about the relationship which should exist between a club and the mutual founded by its supporters.

It is right to say that the Supporters Direct initiative was born in an atmosphere of mild resentment or even open hostility from supporters towards their clubs. It is also right to say that the immediate reaction of the clubs to supporters seeking involvement and representation at Board level was not sympathetic. However, there are grounds for optimism.

Firstly, it makes good business sense for a club to have a positive relationship with its supporters and the advantage of a truly democratic, not-for-profit mutual is that it is truly representative and can be a focus for sensible discussion of issues. My own view is that the Crystal Palace Supporters' Trust's membership of 4,000 may prove to be a more significant factor in its success in influencing the club than its cash mountain. If a supporters' group is properly organized and has worthwhile aims, any sensible club management will eventually talk to it.

Secondly, the ability of a supporters group to raise significant sums of money for investment at the club will be a big factor in some cases. Supporters may be prepared to contribute to a mutual which is run on a proper basis and makes decisions about spending democratically where they would not contribute to the club itself.

Thirdly, and perhaps slightly worryingly, the satellite, cable and Internet companies which are investing huge sums in football see clubs as a means of access to groups of supporters who may buy their products and services. A well-organized mutual with a large membership will be well placed to bargain for the things it wants in any market which is created.

CONCLUSION

The legal structure of a supporters' group is important. It safeguards the things that matter to the people who join and gives a proper and credible basis for discussions with the club. But then I would say that – I am a lawyer.

The striking thing is that the groups I have talked to have agreed with me. They have had strong beliefs about the basis on which their group should operate, based on the ideas of 'ownership' I have talked about. They do not want to make money. They want to build bridges between their club and the community it serves. They want to be representative and democratic.

So the legal concepts actually bear some relation to reality, which some may think novel. And the evidence is growing that where a supporters' group gets together and gets it right, they really make a difference to their club.

NOTE

1. K. Jaquiss, 'Football, Fans and Fat Cats: Whose Football Club Is it Anyway?', in S. Hamil, J. Michie, C. Oughton and S. Warby (eds.), *Football in the Digital Age: Whose Game Is it Anyway?* (Edinburgh: Mainstream, 2000).

9

Cherries in the Black: AFC Bournemouth's Journey from Bankruptcy to Rude Health under Supporter Leadership

TREVOR WATKINS

'You sound just like a fan', another chairman commented, half smiling. We had been debating how best the monies from a new television deal for the Football League clubs should be split between the three divisions of the Football League. Deep down I am sure we were both fans in that discussion, both wanting to see every club get enough monies to survive. Regrettably, the vested interests of big business, media and each individual club will often conflict and override what an ordinary fan might think. And deep down, as fans, we would have known what would have been for the good of the clubs we now represent at the lower levels of the Football League. Besuited, business-like and at a chairmen's conference, how on earth could we be seen as 'ordinary' fans?

The 'ordinary' fan. Who is this person on the local omnibus travelling to a game? Changes in soccer over the last decade have dramatically altered the backdrop to the game I have loved all my life. How many of us will often stand in the park watching a meaningless game between two unknown teams, one of thousands of similar games played every day? What a perfect way to spend time on a brisk autumn morning. Each week I still have that mad passion for my side. Every season I share the sheer exhilaration of the rollercoaster ride as we hope for promotion, to avoid relegation and end up in mid-table! Four years ago I found myself leading a campaign to save our local club, AFC Bournemouth. Now I am chairman of the club, one that I have supported since I was a kid. I am a lawyer, businessman and now have to wear a tie to a game (or at least that is what is expected). Me, an ordinary fan? Yes, I think I am. What makes me or anyone else who watches a game any different?

MY FIRST GAME

We all remember our first game. It was a typical grey, cold, February afternoon in 1974 when my dad first dragged me along to watch AFC Bournemouth play.

57

The club had recently changed its name from Bournemouth and Boscombe Athletic to give it a more continental feel – sunny south coast, palm trees and the Riviera touch – it also put us top of the alphabet should that ever become important. It certainly made a difference in early season league tables! We stood on a clapped out old terrace and drank hot Bovril as the old man with the flat cap teetered on a rickety wooden ladder leaning to hang the half-time scores on the board behind us. As he looked one way, we watched and cheered the team on their way to a 1–0 victory over Walsall. In those days we stood in the away end, the bit we could best afford and when home fans could quite happily do so without fear. It may have been a chill winter's day, the football may have been mediocre second division fare but it was good enough to hook me, it was now 'my' team, 'our' team in my hometown. Twenty-seven seasons on, the excitement is still the same.

AFC BOURNEMOUTH'S REBIRTH

Until January 1997, I had watched the club week in week out as a loyal fan, and played the game as often as I could within the confines of my slowly subsiding body. Then with the club £5,000,000 in debt it was announced in January 1997 that bankers were placing it in receivership. Unless a buyer was found its very existence was threatened.

In the past there had always been talk of financial difficulty, rumours of impending doom, and yet on each occasion the undefined problems must have been resolved as the club continued. This time, however, they were for real. Like every other fan, I cared. With legal training, working as a solicitor in the City of London, I found myself with a small group of five other fans leading a campaign to save the club. Six months later we had raised over £500,000, enough with the addition of a loan (from the club's existing bankers!) to buy the club for the town and its fans.[1] We did it without any multi-millionaires.

Our aim, with the takeover now successfully completed, was to turn the club into the local community asset that it should always have been. I stood in the shower one day wondering if I could stand and watch the club that I had followed ebb away. Without any real hope but with much design I was determined. At the core was my belief that the key to the success of the club was to re-establish the link between the club and its fans. It is the most important relationship at any club, at any level: fans and the club working with each other, for the good of the club.

Too often football clubs have been seen as commercial organizations just happening to be part of a town. They are far more than that. A team is a vital part of any community, whether it be professional, semi-professional or amateur. Club staff, players and fans cross borders and boundaries within any community. The club is a focal point. With the right emphasis and direction of effort, a club can be a catalyst for change and reinvigoration of a community. It is a modern view which is attracting growing acclaim. Like any business, it is the fans as clients who really should be listened to if the ailing dinosaurs of the prehistoric game are to have a fulfilling future.

When we began our campaign to save AFC Bournemouth, the club itself, like many, was held in low esteem by its fans, and meant little or nothing to the community at large. It was financially ailing, struggling to compete in the post-*Bosman* era. Whilst new accounting controls and financial restraint would underpin its future existence, I believed the key to future success was the formulation of a strong working relationship between fans and the club. There needed to be a belief within the community about the value of a professional football club to the town.

THE IMPORTANCE OF COMMUNITY INVOLVEMENT AND TEAMWORK

We did not have a multi-millionaire, but we did have five lifelong fans, prepared to give the time and effort to the exclusion of everything else bar their normal jobs, to make a go of saving their club. Commitment and dedication are vital to any group looking to succeed. The effort overtook my life and although there have been many wonderful moments, it has brought events and changes that in a fleeting moment sometimes leave me wishing things had been different for me personally. These thoughts soon subside when I can look and see the wider impact of what has happened for the town and community. If you, too, follow a similar road then above all it is the team spirit, the strength of your group that will be important if you are to succeed. Any group of fans will quickly find that there will be those who welcome differing degrees of involvement in the project. Of the thousands who attend on a Saturday afternoon a small minority will want to give their time to become fully involved in their club. A larger number might be prepared to join a supporters' organization to find out more about their club. The greater part of a crowd is more concerned about the winning and losing on the pitch, whilst a community will merely be aware to some degree that a football club exists within the town. Beyond that, there will be many thousands for whom a club means little or nothing at all.

The success of any supporters' group also depends on how the individuals within it divide the responsibilities. As with any business or team, each part will have different strengths. We learned quickly that it was important to play to the skills of each individual member, dividing up responsibilities according to who was most able to deal with the media, administration, fundraising, accounting, and so on. Above all, supporters' groups need to be adaptable. Mistakes will be made, situations will develop, but if each individual is open, honest and trustworthy, then the supporters' group has a strong foundation to build upon. The traditional view within the game is that supporters' groups cannot do anything significant. A failure to be open and honest and reveal past problems will be fatal to the credibility of a supporters' group should any individual member be found to have an unsavoury past. One can ill afford to damage the credibility of not only the individual but also the supporters' group itself. It can seriously set back any progress that may have been made. Honesty, integrity, trust and loyalty: these are the vital requirements for any group.

Fans' bodies will find that their aims and expectations differ. It is important at the outset to know what these are. A key to success for any business is to keep its aim understandable, clear and achievable. Whilst at Bournemouth the aim was a complete takeover, other clubs may seek to have an elected supporter on the board, regular meetings with the board, or to take a shareholding. It is far better to have an achievable aim and objective rather than an unrealizable dream of taking over and running a club. At Bournemouth we were in a rescue situation. No other buyer came forward, we were the only option, and as a rag-tag bunch of supporters we had to prepare ourselves not only to take a stake in the club, but also to run it.

The pioneers of supporters' involvement have shown that supporters can be organized and professional. They must be so if they are to be taken seriously. A basic structure and organization are vital to the success of any supporters' group. For any relationship between a club and its supporters to work, it is important that there is one voice, one group representing all supporters' interests at a club. If more than one voice is heard, it dilutes the effect, and makes it difficult for the club to choose how to take the relationship with its supporters forward.

A group must also decide the message it wishes to convey. Having a responsible and accountable part to play in the life of a club is not met by prolonged criticism and continued pressure for change. More often than not, supporters will not own or have the chance to purchase a majority stake in their club. In that situation, progress, development and fruitful involvement will only be achieved if the method is constructive and proactive rather than destructive and reactive.

SUPPORTER INVOLVEMENT AT BOARD LEVEL: A NEW DAWN

Encouraging supporters to play a greater role in their club is an idea that in the past may have drawn knee-jerk reactions from directors resistant to the idea. Why? Because it has been seen as a 'revolutionary' concept seeking to overthrow kingdoms and bring down boards. That is clearly not the case now. We are seeing a welcome air of support across the game for responsible and accountable involvement by fans in the game. It is understandable that chairmen, directors and majority shareholders are more likely than not initially to resist any move if it is driven by a desire to effect change by removing a chairman, board or shareholder. I very much hope that gone are the days when the idea of responsible supporter involvement was met with derision. I want to see an end to the view that supporters should be just on the terraces on a Saturday afternoon, paying their money but having neither the right to be involved, nor the ability to make any useful contribution to the running of their club. Those views are outmoded, outdated and now overtaken by the events at Bournemouth, Northampton, Luton and other clubs. Supporters have shown that by acting responsibly they can enhance and benefit the club and also the position of a chairman, a board and a shareholder.

As a chairman I have certainly found a new willingness from other club officials to work toward greater supporter integration. To effect change supporters need to build a relationship with the existing owner. A relationship of trust will only be built if both the club and its supporters are prepared to work together to learn and to share a common aim – the enhancement of the club, both on and off the field. It is vital for supporters' groups to develop a relationship of that type, not only with the club, but also with the media. The media love to generate news they can then cover. Conflagration, contradiction and confrontation lend themselves to good stories. However, diplomacy is what will serve supporters best if they are to play a long-term part in the operation of their club.

THE RESPONSIBILITY OF HIGH FINANCE

Perhaps the biggest problem facing any supporter involved in their club is that of big business. The advent of substantial corporate investment in modern professional sport has changed the foundations of each sport that has been touched. Football is no exception. As wages have spiralled in the Premier League, so the demands placed on lower division clubs have also grown significantly. Fees paid by broadcasters for live television coverage go for the most part to the Premier League. Significant sums do drip down to the First, Second and Third divisions. These at least go some way to taming the monster the increased money in the game has created. Whereas 26 years ago it would have cost 35p to stand at Dean Court, now I would have to part with £12.50 for a place on the same ageing terracing.

The decisions affecting any business revolve around being able to pay wages and survival, then looking to growth and expansion. As fans we would love to keep our players, reduce prices and ensure promotion each season. In being involved at our clubs we move from being passionate observers with no formal responsibilities, to interested supporters with very real and substantial responsibilities and accountability. Our decisions become more informed, less about judgements from the sideline on whether the No.3 is good enough or not! Involvement can create a tension between being a fan on the terrace with no consequence for thoughts about the club and the fan 'in the boardroom' who chooses a responsible role in their club. At heart, both want to see their club succeed. In reality each may have a different view on what exactly that means.

As leisure activities have become more varied and the choices available considerably more far reaching, soccer has seen substantial increases in ticket prices, as clubs try to fuel the furnace and meet the soaring costs of employing players. For many clubs, particularly in the Premier League, the increased ticket prices have pushed the game beyond the traditional fan. Football has quickly become a middle-class game, for those who can afford middle-class prices. I have no doubt that for many lower division clubs the money generated by television coverage just about keeps them afloat as the storm of wage demands rages around them. It is a tragedy that the cost has been to distance many ordinary supporters from the game, an effect that could imperil any club with an urgent need to call on its supporters to help it survive. Far better prepared will be the clubs which build those bridges now.

CONCLUSION

Both the Premier League and Football League are working hard to enhance relationships between clubs and their supporters. If supporters' groups can deliver themselves as responsible and accountable organizations, it is in a club's business interest to work with those groups, particularly to develop its product. In doing so, it helps to re-establish the credibility of football clubs within their communities, and assist in properly placing football as a product that benefits.

To date, the gloss of football presents it as a multi-million pound business, paying high wages to foreign legions who appear as movie stars on television each week. Improving and enhancing the relationship between clubs and supporters will at least begin to bring the game back to the people who have sustained it throughout the last century. Listening, hearing and understanding the views of supporters must be fundamental to the future success of the game. For each individual supporter who chooses to play a greater part in their club, however, it will necessarily draw them further away from being an ordinary fan. Instead they must be prepared to become more a person who has to attempt to balance the needs of running a club in the modern game, against the desire to reduce prices, keep the best players, produce success on the field and win every game.

Perhaps the most valuable lesson I have learned is that by becoming involved with my club I can no longer be the ordinary fan. With my fellow directors, all lifelong supporters of the game, we must make decisions for the long-term good of our club, such as selling a player or raising prices. We also have to keep a more careful watch on any comments made during the course of a game now that we have a position of responsibility.

Many hold up Bournemouth as a shining example. I am proud to have led a successful campaign to save the club. Now, almost four years on, we have a strong board, a growing Independent Supporters' Association, and substantive plans for a new share issue to widen ownership of the club throughout the community. We have had to trade without an overdraft, reduce debt and yet still try to retain a semblance of a successful side. We have made mistakes, and have also had great successes. We have become a community flagship, recognized for the work we do, and we are also now a serious voice within football.

I always doubted whether individuals could make a difference. The answer is that they can, so long as they bind together with others of like mind. Four years ago I was enjoying a successful career in the City, a happy home life and the prospect of an excellent career path. What had first appeared to be a minor decision to work toward helping my club to survive turned my life on its head. After years of insurance litigation, I now find my time increasingly taken up with sports law work. I have had the privilege of seeing my team play at Wembley, to play there myself, and also to write a book. I had the pleasure of developing extensive media work, yet still attempt to kick a ball around on a Thursday night when my legal firm's team plays clients.

Above all, my colleagues and I have shown that fans can make a difference. Yes, you have to put yourself second and the project first, but the rewards are significant – not personally, but for the club, and for the community. When we started out, who would have thought that an ordinary bunch of supporters drawn together more by luck than design might just pull their club back from the abyss? We did, but not without the help of many hundreds and thousands of other fans. Quite clearly, the time for supporter participation in clubs has arrived.

This mission has overtaken my life. It led me first to move away from my career in the City, then to work closer to home and now to have an increasing role in a game I love and one where above anything else I can see real, tangible benefits from the ideas now being acted upon. In the last four years I have been privileged to have this opportunity and am now proud to be a member of the core group of Supporters Direct. This is an extension of the supporter philosophy emblazoned at the likes of Bournemouth, Luton and Northampton Town, and my hope is for this to be repeated at many other clubs.

I, chairman, lawyer and businessman, an ordinary fan? Most definitely, but why 'ordinary'? It is the fans who are extraordinary, it is they who are the foundation of any club and it is their involvement that can ensure a vibrant future for any club willing to build a constructive, fruitful relationship with its own.

NOTE

1. For a fuller account of the rescue of AFC Bournemouth from bankruptcy see T. Watkins, *Cherries in the Red: How One Football Fan Saved His Club and became Chairman* (London: Headline, 1998).

10

Shareholders United Against Murdoch

MICHAEL CRICK

The organization Shareholders United sprang from when I was woken up horribly early one Tuesday morning in September 1998 – at least it was horribly early for me, about quarter to nine – by Richard Hytner, who is the chairman of an advertising agency called Publicis. I had known Richard at Manchester Grammar School, 20 years ago in the mid-1970s. We had acted in plays together, but subsequently lost touch until a friend brought us together at a Proms concert and dinner the year before – in 1997 – when Richard had reminded me he was a United supporter and the proud owner of 6,000 shares.

Richard was blunt. The day before, I had made public my opposition to BSkyB's proposed takeover of Manchester United, both in an 'op-ed' article in the London *Evening Standard* and with an opinion-film on *Newsnight*. Was I interested, Richard asked, in setting up a shareholder campaign to fight the takeover? Foolishly perhaps, I immediately said 'Yes'. Richard rang another Old Mancunian, Richard Lander, a former journalist who is now in corporate public relations. I rushed off to Companies House to get a copy of the share register. Richard recruited several others from the advertising world, and quickly found a sponsor willing to give us more than £10,000. The donor wanted to remain anonymous. I told Richard not to tell me who it was – because, as a journalist myself, I cannot resist talking to journalists – but I did ask him one question. Would it embarrass us if it ever got out who it was? It was not Francis Lee, for example. Richard assured me that it would not be embarrassing.

That afternoon we announced our presence to the world, calling ourselves Shareholders United Against Murdoch – or SUAM – and we got a surprising amount of coverage in the following day's papers. From the start we decided to work in conjunction with IMUSA – the unofficial Independent Manchester United Supporters' Association, and I struck up a quick friendship with the IMUSA chairman Andy Walsh. It was all rather amusing, since 15 years before Andy had been a member of the Militant tendency, whilst I probably more than any other journalist had been the person who exposed Militant for what they were. Fortunately no journalist cottoned on to this strange alliance.

There had long been talk of a United shareholders' organization, but nothing had ever come of it. Individuals attended the company's Annual General Meetings and asked awkward questions from time to time, but there was no attempt at coordination. IMUSA had made efforts at forming a share club, but many in IMUSA objected in principle to the 1991 reconstruction of Manchester United – usually called its flotation – which had led to most shares falling into the hands of institutional investors, and therefore ownership of United no longer being with United supporters. It was this of course which made United easy prey to takeover. Many active United fans had principled and ideological objections to owning shares – some still do.

SUAM's view was that there were hundreds of United shareholders out there with a wide range of skills that could be channelled into opposing the BSkyB bid – PR people, journalists, lawyers, bankers, accountants and people from advertising. If we organized ourselves properly we could mount effective, articulate, impassioned but professional opposition to the takeover, which many assumed was a foregone conclusion. Our adversary – the Murdoch empire – was formidable, but not as formidable as we feared. Their handling of the takeover was a PR disaster by them, a model for students at business schools of how not to handle a takeover, from the moment at the famous press conference when BSkyB's American chief executive Mark Booth admitted to not being able to name the United left back. At the subsequent public meeting organized by SUAM and IMUSA I was to suggest that he probably thought that the Neville brothers were a Chicago blues band, that Best, Charlton and Law were a firm of Manhattan attorneys, and that King Eric was a brand of Icelandic condoms.[1]

For the next seven months we were at war, with two aims. First, to put up the strongest possible legal case before the Office of Fair Trading (OFT), to persuade them to recommend that the Secretary of State for Trade and Industry refer the case to the Monopolies and Mergers Commission (MMC),[2] and following the success of this step, to then make as convincing a case as possible to the MMC itself. That involved finding the best competition lawyers, and in the end we recruited several top academics to our cause, and City lawyers, including Peter Crowther, an expert in competition law.

Second, we set out to persuade United shareholders they could vote against the bid, since United and BSkyB had issued a highly misleading Offer Document suggesting that shareholders had no option but to accept BSkyB's offer. It would be almost impossible to persuade institutional shareholders, who held 60 per cent of the shares, or members of the board who together owned a further 17 per cent (mostly accounted for by Martin Edwards who stood to gain £80 million plus a seat on the board of BSkyB). But we had high hopes of the 23 per cent of shares owned by individuals, the overwhelming majority we assumed would be United fans. Our target was to retain at least ten per cent of the shares. BSkyB could only force all shareholders to sell their shares if more than 90 per cent of shareholders accepted the offer. If we got more than ten per cent to say 'No' then those people would be able to hold on to their shares. United could not simply be swallowed whole by the Murdoch empire – it would be forced to remain as a separate company, with its own company accounts and AGMs, and with us as shareholders. We could then carry on fighting from within to maintain at least a limited degree of independence for the football club.

In the end of course, we never needed to undertake that battle to retain the ten per cent shareholding. We had written to all shareholders in preparation, and had urged them not to accept the offer. But as soon as the bid had been referred to the Monopolies and Mergers Commission, all the acceptances that BSkyB had received for their offer became null and void. The best they could hope for was to be given a go-ahead to make a renewed bid. However, the Monopolies and Mergers Commission and Stephen Byers then blocked the bid. Nevertheless, in future that ten per cent figure may still prove important.[3] So long as it looks as if shareholders holding ten per cent of the shares will vote to hang on to their shares no matter what the price, then it acts as a significant deterrent against any future bids, which after all are costly affairs.

GOODBYE SUAM – HELLO SHAREHOLDERS UNITED

Once we had won, SUAM reformed itself on a formal basis, with a proper Constitution, elected – or press-ganged – committee and officers, and we called ourselves simply Shareholders United (SU). The broad aim of SU is to represent the interests of shareholders who are fans of the club, to work to maintain the club's independence, and to encourage wider share ownership among supporters – in line with one of the board's own stated aims at the time of the 1991 flotation. Our philosophy is that the more fans own shares, and the more shares they own, then the harder it will be for an outsider to take over the club. But we are also realistic enough to know that other takeover bids are possible, especially when three-quarters of the shares are now owned by institutions which are not committed to United in the same way fans are. We have tried to establish a position – and in my view we have succeeded already – whereby next time anyone wants to buy United, they will at least talk to us first.

SU has achieved an astonishing amount since we were formed in May 1999, on the day United took the League title, beating Spurs 2–1 at Old Trafford. Originally the board refused to have anything to do with us – perhaps not surprising given our role in opposing the BSkyB bid, which they had welcomed and supported. When we asked to meet the board to discuss the future of United, the company chairman Professor Sir Roland Smith wrote back to us saying that he did not think it right to meet one small group of shareholders and told us to raise any points we had at the Annual General Meeting in November.

So we checked the law and found how surprisingly easy it is to put down a motion at the AGM. In our case we needed just 100 signatures representing 100,000 shares between them. Well, SU now has more than 700 members with almost two million shares. So we gathered the signatures and put down two motions, one calling on the board to recognize us and talk to us about ways of promoting share ownership among fans. The second proposed that the company implement a dividend reinvestment scheme. Many fan shareholders had always been unhappy with the idea of taking cash dividends out of the club – our view was that we should not make money out of United, and that instead all dividends should be ploughed back into the club. The Dividend Reinvestment Plan enables shareholders to take their dividend in the form of extra shares instead of cash, and our hope is that this will mean that over time the proportion of shares owned by fans will gradually increase, as the institutions take the cash dividends and the supporters take the additional shares.

And legally we were not just allowed to submit our motions for the AGM, we were also entitled to then write 1,000-word statements for inclusion in the agenda sent to all shareholders explaining who we were and what were our arguments in favour of the motions. Simply putting two motions down on the agenda for the AGM seemed to send some of the directors into apoplexy. It had never happened before. In fact so far as I can gather it is indeed pretty rare that anyone submits any resolutions to the AGM of a public company. And the board seemed to regard it as a supreme embarrassment.

The board insisted that they would have to oppose both motions. First, they argued, they could not treat any one group of shareholders any differently from any other. Second, they said they could not promote wider share ownership in United, as there were important legal restrictions on a company promoting its own shares. And third, there was no need for the resolution on the Dividend Reinvestment Plan since they planned to do that anyway. Sources inside the club told us that they had only agreed to implement the scheme as a result of us suggesting it – but that they would not admit this publicly as it would only give us credence.

But what also worried the board was the prospect of an acrimonious debate at the November 1999 AGM. Suddenly, from refusing to talk to us, we received feelers through United's PR agency, asking if we would meet Sir Roland ahead of the AGM to try and settle our differences. We replied 'Yes, of course' and at that meeting Sir Roland agreed that he would announce at the AGM that in future SU would be treated along the same lines as are the institutional shareholders. We would receive the same briefings other institutions get. And if we could work out ways of promoting share ownership legally among United fans, then they would meet us to consider our proposals.

So although the board strongly urged all shareholders to vote against our motions, and they were duly voted down at the AGM, we did effectively get everything that we had been asking for. In the circumstances, we also received a surprisingly large number of votes for our resolutions, with around 20 per cent of votes being in favour. From being a quasi-guerrilla organization fighting the BSkyB bid and our own board's attempt to sell our club, we had come to be treated as not only respectable but also seen to have a legitimate right to be consulted over the future of United.

LESSONS LEARNED

Our experience shows that with good organization and the proper use of professional skills, individual fan shareholders can achieve a great deal by working together collectively. Above all, we have made full use of the media. Newspapers, radio and television are hungry for stories about United. We have had no difficulty in making our voice heard, most recently illustrated by our call in 2000 for a proper full-time spin-doctor to sort out United's PR problems. Calling for better PR was a tricky issue for us – for a spin doctor would actually make our lives as a pressure group that much harder. But the fiasco of the Club World Championship in Brazil had been the final straw in what many recognize is an appalling PR operation at Old Trafford. It culminated in Martin Edwards being caught by the *Daily Mirror* with a prostitute – the woman even told the paper how Edwards was worried journalists might find them together. There was a certain inevitability about the whole sorry episode.

Our organization has become one of the first ports of call for reporters covering all sorts of stories relating to United. Of course, this situation is not typical for supporters' groups – we are in a privileged position in the sense that newspapers, radio and television are hungry for stories about United to the point of obsession. But I think that shareholders in any football club will find it relatively easy to get coverage for their views, in comparison, for example, to the shareholders of a company of similar size in any other field, especially if they are voiced intelligently and professionally. Use of the media is a huge advantage we have as football shareholders, along with the other tools outlined above – causing a fuss at an Annual General Meeting, and putting motions down on the agenda. Fan shareholders can potentially exert a lot more influence than fans that are not shareholders of the club. In our case we have the best of both worlds, in that we work closely with the Independent Manchester United Supporters' Association.

As for the future, the Manchester law firm Cobbetts is working on a revised constitution for our organization that will allow us to buy and hold shares on behalf of others. This will allow Shareholders United to make a single large purchase of shares each month, thus practically eliminating the dealing costs which are otherwise prohibitive for small purchases. This in turn will permit the launch of two important initiatives. Firstly, at present, we can only recruit existing shareholders. There are plenty of others who support the aims of our organization but who do not actually own shares. The club's Manchester stockbroker makes a minimum charge of £50 for buying shares, so it is not only time consuming but also expensive. With our new constitution we will be able to recruit anyone for £10, half of which will go to pay the annual subscription and the other half will purchase a single share in the club which will be held by us (in a 'Nominee Account') on behalf of that member. This should allow a huge increase in recruitment.

Secondly, it will allow us to launch a monthly saving scheme. Members will pay a monthly standing order (or cheque, credit card payment or cash), with practically the whole of the monthly amount going to buy shares to be held on behalf of each individual, again with practically no dealing costs since we will be making a single payment for the one purchase, and spreading it over what we hope will be several thousand participants.

These two initiatives should lead to a big increase both in the number of Shareholders United members and also in the size of our collective share holding. We are currently exploring with lawyers and Supporters Direct to what extent we can get the Football Club to assist us in these initiatives, despite the law, which prevents companies promoting their own shares. If necessary we hope to be able to work with Supporters Direct to investigate whether and how the law might be changed.

Finally, we will continue to seek to represent the views of genuine Manchester United fans to the board. Above all, should any other major company ever think of bidding for United in the future as BSkyB did in the past then I have absolutely no doubt that we have already succeeded in establishing ourselves sufficiently well to know that at the very least any such company would realize that they should consult us first before launching what would be an expensive operation. And were they to fail to consult us, I would say that their operation might well be defeated. In the event of another bid like the one from BSkyB, we would be much better equipped and much more prepared and organized than we were last time. They would launch a bid in the face of opposition from United fans at their peril.

NOTES

1. For an inside story of the whole campaign, including this public meeting, see A. Brown and A. Walsh, *Not for Sale! Manchester United, Murdoch and the Defeat of BSkyB* (Edinburgh: Mainstream, 1999). A separate account, focusing more on the issues than the campaign, is provided by S. Lee, 'The BSkyB Bid for Manchester United Plc', in S. Hamil, J. Michie and C. Oughton (eds.), *A Game of Two Halves? The Business of Football* (Edinburgh: Mainstream, 1999).
2. Subsequently renamed the Competition Commission.
3. For a detailed discussion of the reasons behind the rejection of the BSkyB bid for Manchester United see: P. Crowther, 'The Attempted Takeover of Manchester United by BSkyB', in S. Hamil, J. Michie, C. Oughton and S. Warby (eds.), *Football in the Digital Age: Whose Game is It Anyway?* (Edinburgh: Mainstream, 2000); N. Finney. 'The MMC's Inquiry into BSkyB's Merger with Manchester United plc', in S. Hamil *et al.* (eds.), *Football in a Digital Age*; Brown and Walsh, *Not for Sale!*; and Monopolies & Mergers Commission (MMC), *British Sky Broadcasting plc and Manchester United plc: A Report on the Proposed Merger* (CM 4305) (London: Stationery Office, 1999).

11

The Celtic Trust

PETER CARR, JEANETTE FINDLAY, SEAN HAMIL,
JOE HILL and STEPHEN MORROW

For the last year the authors have been among a group of Celtic Football Club supporters who have come together to establish a supporter-shareholder trust at the club. In September 2000 this organization took legal form through the registration of an Industrial and Provident Society with the Registrar of Friendly Societies in Edinburgh. The title of the new organization is 'The Celtic Supporters' Society Ltd', otherwise known as The Celtic Trust.

The registration of The Celtic Trust will make it one of the first of the new breed of supporter-shareholder trusts to be established in the UK. And while its Scottish base has meant that The Celtic Trust has been unable to benefit directly from assistance from Supporters Direct, whose remit covers only England and Wales, it has benefited from advice and support from some of the prime movers in the Supporters Direct initiative, most notably Jonathan Michie, Brian Lomax and Kevin Jaquiss.[1]

However, as this essay will demonstrate, the idea of forming a supporter-shareholder trust at Celtic is not a new one and indeed pre-dates the establishment of Supporters Direct. In fact the whole issue of the establishment of such trusts has been a live issue in Scottish football for a number of years, notably at Hamilton Academicals and Dundee United. The United for Change group at Dundee United has campaigned very vigorously in this regard and the fans at Hamilton received a very respectable vote when they fielded a candidate in a 1999 parliamentary by-election in the town to highlight their campaign. There also exists a Scottish-wide dimension. The Scottish Independent Supporters Coalition (SISCO), a loose coalition of fan groups who are trying to achieve more say in the running of their clubs, has representatives from fans of approximately 15 clubs involved in senior football in Scotland and are lobbying for the establishment of a Supporters Direct organization for Scotland.

In the recent history of Celtic, large numbers of individual supporters (around 15,000 in fact) bought shares in the club which collectively left them with a very high proportion of the voting rights (between 35 per cent and 50 per cent depending upon the estimate). This phenomenon together with the historical roots of the club – rooted in community self-help, social welfare provision and a vehicle for the expression of community pride – all combined to make the formation of a supporter-shareholder trust a particularly appropriate form whereby Celtic fans could exercise influence in their club.

The road to the establishment of a supporter-shareholder trust at Celtic has been a long and difficult one and there is still some way to travel. However, some progress has been made. The authors have taken this opportunity to record their experiences by way of illustration of the potential pitfalls that lie ahead for other putative supporter-shareholder groups who intend following this road.

SOME HISTORY

Celtic Football Club is one of the proudest names in world football. The first team from the United Kingdom to win the European Cup, in 1967, the club has always had a reputation for playing flamboyant, exciting, attacking football in the finest traditions of the 'beautiful game'.

However, the club has always had a wider significance for its supporters than simply as a purveyor of, sometimes, top class football. Critically it acts as a pivotal source of cultural identity. This has made it, in the words of the motto of that other famous European football institution FC Barcelona, 'More than a Club' to its many supporters. As the then Celtic Plc (the holding company for the Celtic Football and Athletic Company Ltd) chairman Frank O'Callaghan acknowledged in the 1998/1999 *Annual Report*, 'As Celtic develops as a football club and a business, it is important to remember its impact as a social institution and the responsibilities that carries.'[2] In this regard Celtic Plc has one of the most developed community involvement programmes of any UK football club via its Celtic Charity Fund,[3] something from which its supporters would take some pride.[4]

In order to understand the special community dimension of Celtic it is necessary to know a little about its history.[5] Celtic Football Club was established by Brother Walfrid, a member of the Catholic Marist order, in 1888. He had two aims. Firstly, he wished to raise funds to provide food for the poor of the East End of Glasgow, many of whom were Irish Catholic immigrants. But secondly, he wanted to create a vehicle to bring together the newly arrived Irish and the indigenous Scottish Protestant, population. So, the Marist brother sought for the Club to have both a Scottish and Irish identity and hence, the Club's name 'Celtic' came about, representing a bridge of cultures across the Irish Sea. A driving force in the emergence of Celtic was the notion of mutual self-help. Glasgow's Irish community wished to establish a welfare system through which they could demonstrate that they could look after themselves and that they would not act as a drain on the wider community's resources. One interpretation of the willingness of Celtic supporters in the 1990s to subscribe for shares in such large numbers is that it is but the latest manifestation of this instinct for self-help in the tradition of mutual organization and the co-operative ideal.

In 1892 Celtic moved to their current home at Parkhead in the East End of Glasgow. The centre-square of turf in the ground was made up of shamrocks from County Donegal in the north-west of Ireland, a county with a particularly strong history of emigration to Scotland, and Glasgow in particular. The famous Irish social radical and labour activist Michael Davitt laid the centre square. Brought up in Lancashire of County Mayo parents, Davitt lost an arm in an industrial accident in a spinning mill at the age of nine. Nevertheless, he went on to form the Irish Land League with the leader of the Irish Parliamentary Party at Westminster, Protestant landowner and social reformer Charles Stewart Parnell. The Land League ultimately won the right for Irish tenant farmers to own their own land through the Wyndham Land Acts of the early twentieth century. In his non-sectarianism, social radicalism and pride in his Irish culture and tradition Davitt exactly embodied the proud traditions that have come to embody Celtic as a social institution, a tradition maintained through its ongoing initiative to combat racism and sectarianism as set out in its Social Mission Statement.[6]

In football terms, 1965–74 were the glory years for Celtic. Under the management of the incomparable Jock Stein the club won nine Scottish League Championships in a row (and a total of 24 major domestic trophies – an average of two trophies every season), won the European Cup in 1967 and reached the final again in 1970 only to be defeated by Feyenoord of Holland.[7] The club remained successful on a more limited scale in the domestic arena into the 1980s. However, in the early 1990s it fell into financial and playing crisis. When Celtic was incorporated as a limited company the majority of share-buyers were businessmen in Glasgow's East End. They were the initiators of lines of succession which survived all the way through to 1994. The lack of dynamism in shareholdings may have contributed to a lack of dynamism in the way the club was run: the Kelly, White and Grant family groupings jealously guarded their control of Celtic while the club squandered the opportunity to build on its extraordinary footballing success. As the football world developed around it, particularly at arch-rivals Rangers, Celtic seemed paralysed. It became apparent that the club management had failed to move with the times. By 1994, riven with internal disputes and allegations of financial and managerial incompetence, and with shareholder and supporter unrest at fever pitch, the club moved to the verge of financial collapse as attendances haemorrhaged.

With the club on the verge of receivership it was saved by the intervention of Scottish-born, but Canadian-based businessman, Fergus McCann, He bought a controlling interest in the club, stabilized its borrowings and introduced a number of other major new investors. A crucial part of McCann's plans was a share issue to ordinary supporters which took place early in January 1995. Some 10,500 supporters took up the opportunity to invest in Celtic raising a total of £9.4m and leaving supporters with in excess of 40% of the shares in Celtic. Subsequently, shares in Celtic Plc, of which the football club was a subsidiary, were listed on AIM (Alterative Investment Market) in September 1995, before being admitted to the main market of the Stock Exchange in September 1998.

Ironically given the club's roots, this was the first time most ordinary supporters had had the opportunity to take a stake in the club they loved. One consequence of this was that there were extremely low levels of secondary market trading of shares in Celtic (for example, a daily average of 0.05 per cent of the number of shares in circulation between 21 September 1998 and 8 April 1999) by comparison with a conventional listed Plc.[8] This is despite the fact that in early 1997 the shares were at one point worth nearly six and a half times the 1995 offer price. Even in August 2000 shares purchased in 1995 were still worth approximately three and half times their original offer price. Clearly supporters had not invested primarily for capital gain. Certainly their behaviour could not be described as that of conventional profit-maximising investors. A much more profound and deeply emotional relationship was at work here than a simple desire to realize a speculative capital gain.

McCann then initiated a five-year programme of rebuilding. The club's Parkhead ground was almost entirely reconstructed, and Celtic won the Scottish League Championship in the 1997/98 season, after a nine-year barren streak. By the beginning of the 1999/2000 season Parkhead had become the largest club stadium in the UK with a capacity of nearly 60,000, and 53,388 season ticket-holders. Interest in the club was also rejuvenated: average home attendances increased from 25,347 in the 1994/95 season to 56,223 in 1998/99.[9] Matters had also taken a turn for the better financially. Turnover almost quadrupled in the 1994–99 period, having largely stagnated under the old regime.

In autumn 1999 Fergus McCann made good on his promise to sell his 51 per cent shareholding in the club. Not only that, but he decided to sell his stake to the existing shareholders and season ticket-holders. This was a radical step. By way of contrast, when Martin Edwards sold a significant part of his then controlling interest in Manchester United in October 1999 for £41m, he sold direct to institutional investors in the City of London. He bypassed the significant number of small shareholders in Manchester United and the club's season ticket-holders. Fergus McCann explained his decision to open up the possibility of owning a share in the club to a wider group of supporters when he told the *Daily Record* on the 7th October 1999:

> I believe it is important the ordinary supporters have a say in the running of their club. Celtic cannot end up like Manchester United who are [majority] owned by institutions ... Celtic Football Club itself is an institution, which should not be in the hands of one individual or the City. The supporters must make sure they can make their voice heard in the boardroom and they can only do that by buying shares. I am stepping back now – the supporters have a chance to fill my shoes.[10]

As Morrow explains, given the large number of supporters who had already bought shares in the 1995 offer, and given that it might be argued that unlike conventional financial investment there existed little incentive to increase the level of one's emotional investment if one already held shares, many observers were sceptical that such a transfer of shares to the supporters could work.[11] In fact the sale was a resounding success. Despite a minimum investment of £700 being required, subscriptions were received for just over 75 per cent of McCann's shares generating a sum of just over £20m. Celtic now has 16,000 supporter-shareholders. Immediately after the sale in November 1999, the largest single shareholder was Irish businessman Dermot Desmond with a stake of 19.8 per cent, while institutional investors had a stake of approximately 17 per cent. Of the remainder, between 35 per cent and 50 per cent of the shares are owned by small supporter-shareholders, depending on how the term 'small' is defined, with the balance held by a number of high net-worth individuals. However it is also the case that many of these individuals who own large tranches of shares also bought for emotional reasons. When preference shares, issued at the time of the 1995 shares, are converted into ordinary voting shares in June 2001 it is a possibility that the small supporter-shareholders could gain a controlling interest. Irrespective of the precise percentage holdings, what is indisputable is that Celtic supporters now have the potential for a more powerful voice than at any other club in Britain. With the club's history and social and community significance it is perhaps fitting that it is Celtic which has the best opportunity to establish a formal and structured relationship between the club and its fans through a supporter director and this can be implemented through the Celtic Trust.

For many Celtic supporters Fergus McCann remains a controversial figure whose frequently abrupt and pugnacious manner made him many enemies. What is incontrovertible is that under his leadership Celtic was successfully re-built as an institution and put on a sound financial footing to an extent that would have seemed scarcely credible in the dog days of the early 1990s. Critically, McCann also made good on his commitment to give Celtic's army of supporters a chance to cement their sense of emotional ownership of the club with a real financial purchase. Extraordinarily, given the tortured internal politics and litany of unfulfilled promises that characterized Celtic's administration in the early 1990s, Fergus McCann did exactly what he said he would. In doing so he threw down the gauntlet to Celtic's supporters and posed the question: do Celtic supporters want to turn ownership into influence over the way their club is managed and developed?

PROBLEMS WITH PLCs

The concept that football clubs are not conventional businesses and are essentially social institutions is not new.[12] However, until recently the ownership structure of most clubs has precluded any form of more inclusive supporter involvement. As was exactly the case at Celtic, football clubs tended to be owned and controlled by influential local business people, such as the Kellys, Whites and Grants, who saw their involvement in the club as an extended form of social obligation or *noblesse oblige*. While this structure of ownership worked well for most of this century, by the 1980s it was becoming obvious that it was no longer appropriate. Critically this structure made it difficult to raise funds to modernize stadiums and invest in wider commercial activities. In any case the various ownership dynasties around the country had lost their commercial vitality and, in most cases, were simply presiding over a slow but steady decline of their clubs. One way to address this problem was to take the route ultimately chosen by Celtic after Fergus McCann bought his stake in the club, and over 20 clubs in England; listing on the Stock Exchange and the adoption of public limited company structure.

However, there is a major difficulty with the move toward Stock Exchange-listed Plc status by football clubs. Essentially the creation of Plc status institutionalizes the pursuit of profit as the core *raison d'être* of the organization. This is because the core obligation of the commercial managers of any Plc is to serve the financial interests of their shareholders. As has been well documented elsewhere, and is starkly illustrated in Celtic's case by the extraordinarily low levels of turnover in Celtic Plc's shares mentioned above, the reality is that most football supporters have not bought their shares as a form of financial investment, but as a form of emotional investment.[13] But paradoxically, the drive for profit encourages the club to erode the emotional bond between club and the traditional supporter.

Specifically, Plc status sets in train commercial forces that many argue inevitably over-exploit the goodwill and pockets of football's traditional, core supporters who have the deepest emotional investment in clubs. There is a lot of evidence to support the over-exploitation hypothesis; witness, for example, the 300 per cent increase in ground ticket prices in England over the last ten years.[14] Even observers with only a commercial interest in the game recognize that such over-exploitation may have negative side effects even for them. In an analysis of the financial prospects of publicly quoted UK football teams, investment bank Salomon Brothers describe the concept of 'fan equity', the emotional bond which links fans to their clubs, arguing that it is from this emotional wellspring that the economic power of football clubs flows.[15] Indeed they go so far as to call the 'fan equity' relationship an 'irrational' one, which it certainly is in conventional economic terms. The passion of the supporters in the ground contributes to the spectacle, thus enhancing its value as a television product. And, as research by the English Premier League indicates, because traditional fans are more loyal to their clubs in less successful times than many 'new' fans attracted to the game in its recent television-driven 'entertainment' manifestation, they provide for more even income streams over time;[16] or in the words of Salomon Brothers, 'It is fan equity that decreases the volatility of earnings when the team experiences failure'.[17]

It is important to emphasize that making a distinction between supporters who attend games regularly and those who may only watch games on television is not to denigrate the very genuine interest of the many fans who are unable to attend games for whatever reasons but who still have a genuine love of their respective clubs. However, from an analytical point of view it is necessary to recognize that there has recently emerged a wide range of 'new' fans for whom it is the spectacle as pure entertainment, rather than any more deep-seated emotional attachment, which attracts them to televised football. And this group is particularly coveted by television advertisers and broadcasters. The net effect of exploitative behaviour toward traditional fans may be to destroy 'fan equity' by driving them from grounds to which they may never subsequently return. Again Salomon Brothers point out how the practice of broadcasting US baseball at prime time, because this is the most expensive advertising slot, made it difficult for fans of teams on the US East Coast to follow their team without sacrificing sleep – 'bad news given teenagers and children are tomorrow's supporters'.[18]

If football then becomes just another 'fashion-driven' entertainment business whose main audience is those seeking a primarily entertainment spectacle, along the lines of the World Wrestling Federation event or a rock concert, then it will be much more vulnerable to fickle fashion trends. Critically, the argument goes, it is the fact that football clubs are essentially 'social' institutions that accounts for the extraordinary emotions that they generate, and which sets them apart from conventional entertainment service providers. This is certainly the case at Celtic. Football clubs therefore ideally require a different form of structural organization to a Plc to reflect their unique nature, some form of mutual or co-operative structure, not only to protect their unique status as cultural assets, but to protect their economic generating power as well.

Unfortunately the threat to the social character of football clubs by the adoption of Plc status is very real. This can be seen in the pressures exerted on clubs by the opportunities presented by lucrative television broadcasting contracts, such as the conditions attached to contracts allowing television companies to dictate the day and kick-off time of games. One of the phenomena driving football's financial renaissance in the 1990s was the extraordinary amounts of money that flowed into the game as television companies, notably BSkyB, were prepared to pay enormous sums to purchase broadcasting rights to games. Rapidly, television money became a critical source of revenue, and one which conceivably could outstrip gate money in terms of importance to clubs.[19] Fundamentally this also represented a shift in importance towards fans who primarily watch their club on television, and away from traditional supporters who actually attend games, in terms of significance in revenue terms. The consequences of this are already being seen. At Celtic the re-scheduling of matches at short notice to accommodate television schedules plays havoc with the travel arrangements of the thousands of Celtic fans who travel from Ireland, England and Wales. But as the United States baseball example above illustrates, the experience in US sports markets should not lead us to be surprised by such developments when short-term commercial imperatives dominate, as they inevitably do in companies with a Plc structure.

Although it might sound extraordinary, it has even been argued in some influential quarters that the attendance of traditional fans at games may not even be that important to providing a spectacle. The *Financial Times* reported an example of the surrender to television priorities and where it might lead when it highlighted the use of "canned cheering" by the Scottish Rugby Union during a 1999 rugby world cup match. A spokesperson for the Scottish Rugby Union (SRU) spoke of the need for 'jazzing things up a bit'.[20] In the authors' view, to go down this road is to strip sporting occasions of any social significance and reduce them to the level of purely entertainment spectacles. Some may argue that this is no great loss; but the authors would profoundly disagree with this contention. It is the network of social affinities between supporters and their clubs which give all the great football occasions their real magic, a fact that Salomons were shrewd enough to recognize in their discussion of the 'fan equity' concept. All football clubs, but a club like Celtic in particular, are an essential part of their supporters' shared social and cultural heritage. To reduce the club as an institution to one of solely economic significance, which is how Plc status characterizes and operationalizes strategic goal setting in conventional business firms, will in the long run have the inevitable effect of reducing football clubs and stadiums to the level of theme parks. Celtic, and the clubs like it, in their current form offer something much more vital and deep. And ironically, as Salomons again acknowledge, there is the danger that football clubs' economic success may become more problematic once the social or 'irrational' dimension of clubs is destroyed.[21]

It is, however, important to emphasize that it is not the influx of television monies into the game in itself that is the problem; in fact this influx is to be welcomed, as it allows clubs to re-invest in improving their facilities and services whilst bringing the spectacle of the game to a wider audience. The problem is, on what terms this revenue is channelled into institutions, Plcs, whose fundamental obligation is to their financial shareholders, rather than to the wider social community which was the reason for their foundation in the first place; there is a built-in incentive to prioritize the short-term commercial interests, and these frequently do not match the social imperatives. This is most obviously demonstrated by the way the need for travelling supporters to be sure that match kick-off times are not moved at short notice is over-ridden by the scheduling of television companies. What is required is a firm structure which enables a football club to negotiate the full value of its services from commercial organizations such as television companies while protecting the interests of all its supporters, but which then channels this revenue in the interests of the clubs' supporters and local communities, not just its financial shareholders.

Paradoxically, despite all its shortcomings, Plc status does offer one major advantage. It gives a window of opportunity for fans to exercise some influence over those clubs where supporters hold significant shareholdings. However, as long as fans' shareholdings are dispersed it is difficult for them to express their opinion. What is required is a means to unite all the individual supporter-shareholders in one vehicle to challenge the influence of institutional or high-net-worth individual shareholders. If clubs are bought or effectively controlled by media companies this opportunity will be lost forever. This scenario remains very real despite the Monopolies and Mergers Commission's (MMC) decision to block BSkyB's bid for Manchester United.[22] The BSkyB, NTL and Granada TV companies now hold significant and influential shares in ten out of the 20 English Premier League clubs.

THE GENESIS OF THE CELTIC SUPPORTER-SHAREHOLDER TRUST

Fan disenchantment with the negative effects of the increasing commercialization of football and the erosion of the social purposes of clubs has been well documented.[23] Similarly the opportunities presented by Plc status for fans to exercise more influence has also been noted, particularly in the context of Celtic.[24]

The first attempt to galvanize the collective power of the army of individual supporter-shareholders in Celtic was undertaken in autumn 1997. Heriot-Watt and Edinburgh University CSC (HWEUCSC), one of the largest Celtic supporters clubs in Scotland, resolved to push for a more proactive role for the fans in the running of Celtic. This proposed electing fans onto both the Football Club and Plc boards to represent the ordinary supporter-shareholders. During that season a draft proposal was drawn up by HWEUCSC detailing the mechanisms of how to achieve this. The supporters' club formed a small sub-committee[25] to discuss how to take this forward to both Celtic and its supporters. At the end of the 1997/98 season, with Celtic having just become champions but losing their Dutch coach Wim Jansen, the sub-committee, having dubbed their idea 'Elect-A-Celt', wrote to Fergus McCann, outlining their proposals. There then ensued a lengthy correspondence on the scheme between club member Peter Carr and Fergus McCann. Details of the Heriot-Watt initiative were posted in an article on the *Bhoyzone* Internet site, one of the most popular Celtic Supporter fanzine websites.

In September 1998 HWEUCSC attempted, along with ten other shareholders, to put two resolutions down at the Celtic Plc Annual General Meeting. A combination of timing and lack of familiarity with the detail of company law (to have a resolution discussed at a Plc AGM requires 100 shareholders holding shares to the value of at least £100 each to sign the motion) prevented the two resolutions being formally raised.

In early January 1999 Fergus McCann invited Carr to a meeting in the Celtic boardroom at Celtic Park where the HWEUCSC proposal was discussed. Although McCann disagreed strongly with many of the points raised he did indicate that at the end of his five-year tenure he intended to offer his controlling 51 per cent to the ordinary fans of Celtic. His view was that if the ordinary supporters took up the new share issue in sufficient numbers then they were perfectly entitled to organize into a share block and seek boardroom representation.

As mentioned above, the October 1999 sale of Fergus McCann's shares to existing shareholders and season ticket-holders was a success with McCann netting an estimated £36m. Also in October 1999, at the Celtic AGM Carr called on the Celtic Plc board to take more account of the views and interests of the fans, specifically asking for the AGMs to be moved to weekends and the board to consult with supporters to agree jointly on a scheme to elect fans onto the board. To date Celtic Plc AGMs have been held on Monday mornings. This was clearly not conducive to facilitating the widest possible attendance by supporter-shareholders. At the 1999 AGM the then Plc chairman Frank O'Callaghan lightly dismissed both ideas. This sparked some expressions of anger in the audience.

Independently, the Football Research Unit at Birkbeck College, University of London, along with colleagues in other UK universities including Jeanette Findlay at the University of Glasgow's Department of Urban Studies, had been researching alternative structures for football clubs.[26] This work had been supported by the Co-operative Party[27] which published a pamphlet on the subject.[28] The Co-operative Party had also engaged in lobbying the Labour government on the potential benefits of supporting supporter-shareholder trusts at sports clubs and had organized a meeting on the subject at the Labour Party conference. At that Party conference the Secretary of State for Culture, Media and Sport in England and Wales, Chris Smith MP, announced that the Government was to launch a new initiative to facilitate the setting up of supporter-shareholder trusts.

Following this announcement an informal meeting of interested Celtic supporters was held in Glasgow on 2 December 1999 where all those who had been lobbying for the application of some form of supporter-shareholder democracy at Celtic came together for the first time. The purpose of the meeting was to discuss the long-term feasibility of establishing a mutual/co-operative trust structure at Celtic Plc; and in the short term to create an organizational vehicle by which Celtic supporters could simply exercise more influence over how their club was administered. Through such a structure supporters and shareholders in Glasgow Celtic football club might pool their voting rights in order to provide an institutional framework within which supporters could influence the running of the club. This would allow them to protect the fundamental purpose of the club as a sporting, social and cultural institution. The meeting was held under the auspices of the Co-operative Party in its offices at Bath Street. However, all the individuals attending did so in a personal capacity, and not as representatives of any other organizations.[29]

The meeting decided that there was enough anecdotal evidence to suggest that it was worth proceeding to establish a mutual/co-operative association of supporters and shareholders at Celtic, to be called The Celtic Trust. It was decided to hold a public meeting in Glasgow City Hall on 5 February 2000 to launch the initiative. There was consensus at this initial December meeting on the view that, if it were to be successful, it was important that the Trust approached

Celtic Plc with a positive agenda. The purpose of the Trust was to strengthen the club and not weaken it. So from the very outset it was emphasized that in all its dealings the Trust should be seeking to have a constructive dialogue with the Plc. It was resolved that the Plc be kept informed of all developments, and representatives of the Plc were invited to attend any future meetings. Even when Celtic did not send representatives to any of the meetings, the Trust Secretary ensured that Celtic was kept informed of the outcomes of these meetings and their overall purpose. There was a common view that, while most people did not think that Celtic was being badly managed at that point (certainly not in comparison to other periods in its history) – indeed many of the commercial initiatives by the club were to be welcomed – there was still a need for direct fan involvement in the development of the strategy and policy of the club. This was less of a protest movement and more of a democratic movement.

The point was also made that it was vital that any trust structure that was established was genuinely democratic and did not exclude supporters who had not purchased shares. The meeting agreed that this was critically important and that it would be wrong to allocate voting rights in any trust structure simply according to the number of shares owned. But careful thought needed to be applied as to exactly how such a hybrid structure could be established.

Similarly it was agreed that if the Trust idea was to have any chance of success then it needed to be genuinely inclusive, and representative of all parts of the greater Celtic family. In particular it was agreed that both the Association of Celtic Supporters' Clubs (CSA) and the Affiliation of Celtic Supporters' Clubs, should be involved in the planning and establishment of any trust structure. After the meeting an e-mail address was established, and a draft constitution produced for circulation at the 5 February 2000 meeting.

The inaugural public meeting of The Celtic Trust took place on 5 February 2000 in Glasgow City Hall and was chaired by John McAllion MP/MSP. A crowd of approximately 70 attended and a message of support was read out from the L'Elefant Blau supporters group at FC Barcelona. Representatives from Celtic Plc attended and a lively debate ensued. The organizers judged the event a qualified success. But a number of questions from the floor highlighted the fact that until the Trust presented a draft constitution, it was difficult for potential members to know what they might be signing up to. As a result, following the meeting it was agreed that our first priority was to draft a clear constitutional statement of what the Trust was about. The Manchester firm of Cobbetts solicitors to Supporters Direct in England and Wales and specialists in corporate governance work for the co-operative movement, were contacted and agreed to provide the necessary legal advice.

In the meantime, thousands of leaflets were printed, paid for from a whip-round from among the informal steering group, and handed out at Celtic home games; press releases led to a round of press interviews; contact was made with the various Celtic supporter associations – including the Irish Association – and more experienced members were drafted onto the Trust interim board. It was felt necessary to have the services of knowledgeable people who could provide expert advice but at the same time would understand the overriding social purpose of the initiative. Luckily, within the Celtic support, as with most clubs, there is a wealth of talent and expertise which the fledgling Trust could draw on.

In January 2000, following lobbying by the HWEUCSC, and Celtic's largest and oldest supporters grouping, the Celtic Supporters' Association (CSA), which counts among its membership around 170 individual supporter clubs from around the world representing 10,000 members, unanimously passed a resolution in support of the Trust Initiative.[30]

By Easter 2000 it was felt that sufficient progress had been made to convene another public meeting. The meeting was subsequently held on 20 May 2000 at the Celtic Supporters' Association clubrooms on London Road, Glasgow. This time around 140 people attended. Again a lively discussion ensued, and an interim committee was elected[31] to oversee the work of the Trust until its first AGM in September 2000. The chair reminded the meeting of the key objectives of the Trust:

- To provide a mechanism for the collective purchase of shares through a mutually owned organization which might provide a 'safe haven' for individual shareholders wishing to sell their shares.

- To provide a vehicle by which the collective strength of small shareholders can by harnessed through the use of proxy voting.

- To provide a vehicle by which the wider social objects set out by the Trust in its Statement of Principles might be achieved.

The following 'Statement of Principles' or draft constitution document, which put flesh on these objectives, was approved by the meeting. This document encapsulates the core philosophy and preferred *modus operandi* of the Trust and as such is the definitive statement of the Trust's aspirations. It set the framework for the final draft of the constitution which was approved by the first formal Annual General Meeting (AGM) of the Trust in September 2000.

CONCLUSION

The Celtic Supporters' Society Ltd (The Celtic Trust) was formally registered with the Registrar of Friendly Societies as an Industrial and Provident Society in September 2000. Its first act will be to purchase shares on behalf of its members.

Its second, to present two motions to be debated at Celtic's September 2000 AGM. One of these will relate to the holding of AGMs on a Saturday and the other calls on the board to organize the election of a fan representative to join the

The Celtic Trust

'Statement of Principles'

The Celtic Trust will be an Industrial and Provident Society registered with The Registry of Friendly Societies, 58 Frederick St., Edinburgh EH2 1NB.[1] The business of the Trust is to be conducted for the benefit of the community which Celtic Football Club serves and not for the private financial profit of the Trust's members. Therefore the profits or surpluses of the Trust are not to be distributed either directly or indirectly in any way among members of the Society but shall be applied: a) to maintain prudent reserves; b) on expenditure to achieve the Society's objects, principally the purchase of shares in Celtic Plc (hereinafter Celtic).

In keeping with its philosophy, within its capability the Trust will co-operate with other Supporters' Trusts, co-operatives and their associations at local, national and international levels who share the objects of the Trust.

The final details of the Trust's constitution are currently the subject of discussion between the interim committee of the Trust and its legal advisors, Cobbetts of Manchester. Cobbetts are also legal advisors to the government-sponsored Supporters Direct scheme; Supporters Direct provides advisory support to supporters' groups wishing to establish supporter-shareholder trusts in England and Wales.

The interim committee seeks approval from supporters at this stage of the broad aims and outline structure of the Trust and authority to complete the registration of the Trust with the Registry of Friendly Societies. Once the Trust has been registered, membership will be offered to supporters on the basis set out in this note.

1. Objects

The operating principles of the Trust are founded in the philosophy of co-operation and its central values of equality, equity and mutual self-help. Specifically, the objects of the Trust are as follows:

1.1 To encourage Celtic to take proper account of the interests of its supporters, and of the community it serves, in its decisions;

1.2 To strengthen the bonds between Celtic and the communities it serves and to represent the interests of the community in the running of Celtic;

1.3 To benefit present and future members of the community served by Celtic by promoting, encouraging and furthering the game of football as a recreational facility, sporting activity and focus for community involvement;

---

1. Under the laws governing Industrial and Provident Societies such organizations cannot be described in their official titles as Trusts. The official name of the organization shall thus be 'The Celtic Supporters' Society Ltd'. However The Celtic Supporters' Society Ltd can trade under the name of 'The Celtic Trust' provided this is acknowledged in the small print at the bottom of Celtic Trust's official printed materials. Therefore the name of the organization for business purposes shall be 'The Celtic Trust'.

1.4 To encourage the club to support the community which it serves and to honour the community objectives of the Club's founders: in this regard the Trust accepts and supports the Social Mission statement of Celtic set out in its Charter;

1.5 To promote support for Celtic financially and otherwise;

1.6 To buy and hold shares in Celtic;

1.7 To give supporters a greater opportunity to invest in Celtic;

1.8 To encourage and promote the principle of supporter representation on the board of Celtic and ultimately to be the vehicle for democratic elections to the Board.

2. Governance

2.1 The day-to-day management of the Trust will be entrusted to an Executive Committee ('the Committee') made up of fifteen members, ten elected by the membership and five appointed. The Committee shall consist of:

- the officers of the Committee who will be five in number – The Chairperson, two Vice Chairs, the Secretary, and the Treasurer;
- four members elected and appointed by existing supporters' associations;
- five other elected members;
- an Honorary President.

The existing supporters' associations which would be entitled to appoint one member as their representative, to be elected at the AGMs or delegates' meetings of their own associations and not directly at the Trust AGM are: The Affiliation of Celtic Supporters' Clubs, The Celtic Supporters' Association, The Irish Association of Celtic Supporters' Clubs, and The North American Federation of Celtic Supporters' Clubs.

2.2 The five Officers and the members of the Committee, other than the representative members of the supporter associations mentioned above, will be elected at the inaugural meeting of the Trust and at each subsequent annual general meeting ('AGM') on a one-member-one-vote basis. Officers may be re-elected but may serve for a continuous period of not more than 4 years.

2.3 Certain decisions, including any resolution to be proposed by the Trust at a general meeting of Celtic, will be reserved by the Rules to the members of the Trust. The Rules will provide for decision making in the Trust by postal ballot.

3. How Would the Trust Work

The principle behind the Trust is that 'the whole is worth more than the sum of the parts'. The objective of the Trust is to act as a collective voice on behalf of all of its members. How is this achieved in practice?

3.1 Shareholders are the owners of any company. In return for providing finance to the company through the purchase of shares, company law provides those shareholders with certain rights: e.g. the right to vote at general meetings of the company and the right to receive dividends.

3.2 The Trust's collective voice or influence arises through its entitlement to speak on behalf of shares held by its members in Celtic Plc. This happens in one of two ways. First, through acting as a proxy for those members of the Trust who already own shares in Celtic Plc (i.e. harnessing the ownership rights of individual shareholders), and second, through owning shares in its own right in Celtic Plc. These shares will be held in the name of the Trust, collectively on behalf of all members of the Trust.

3.3 Giving your proxy to the Trust means that you pass your voting rights in respect of the shares that you own as an individual to the Trust. Giving your proxy to the Trust does not alter your legal status as a shareholder in Celtic Plc. It simply allows the Trust to act and vote the shares held by its members on a collective basis, rather than individual shareholder-supporters acting on an individual basis. This assignation does not affect your rights as a shareholder to either receive any dividends declared by Celtic Plc in respect of your shares, or to sell your shares. You continue to hold the share certificate and receive all formal communications from Celtic Plc. What is transferred to the Trust are the voting rights in respect of those shares, not the ownership.

3.4 Anybody who joins *The Celtic Trust* and who owns shares in Celtic Plc will be asked to assign their proxy voting rights in respect of their shares in Celtic Plc to the Trust by assigning proxy forms. Assignation of the proxy voting rights of members is the basis of the collective strength of the Trust. The collective strength of the Trust is applied once policy matters of principle, such as the approval of motions for submission to the AGM of Celtic Plc, have been established via a ballot of all members, or through a show of hands at a meeting of the Trust's members, on a one-member-one-vote basis.

3.5 The agreement to transfer the proxy voting rights to the Trust can be cancelled at any time by providing written confirmation to the Trust's Secretary.

3.6 If the member of the Trust subsequently attends the Celtic Plc AGM then company law dictates that the proxy would automatically become invalid, but it would obviously be expected that all Trust members in attendance would vote in accordance with Trust policy. Trust members would be expected to give 14 days notice to the Secretary of *The Celtic Trust* that they intended to attend in person.

3.7 Where it became known that a Trust member voted against Trust policy at a Celtic Plc AGM they would be expelled from the Trust.

3.8 To summarize: what you give up when you pass your proxy to the Trust is the right to vote those shares. Instead, however, you have the right to vote, on a one-member-one-vote basis, and be heard within the Trust. You remain the legal owner of the shares in Celtic Plc; you remain entitled to sell the shares at any time; you remain entitled to receive any dividend declared by Celtic Plc. In addition, you are entitled to cancel your proxy at any time, though this will mean giving up your membership of the Trust.

3.9 Trust members who are not existing shareholders in Celtic Plc will pay an additional membership fee upon joining the Trust. This fee will be used, along with other available funds, as determined by the Committee, to purchase shares in Celtic Plc. These shares will be held in the name of the Trust, collectively on behalf of all members of the Trust.

4. Individual Purchases of Shares

The Trust will encourage the directors of Celtic to set up a scheme which will make further direct investment by individual supporters in shares in Celtic as affordable and convenient as possible.

other directors. For now, the main aim of the Trust is to have proper representation of fans' interests in Celtic's administration and full accountability at board level.

A long way has been travelled, from a number of different directions, since this issue was first raised. Some may ask why, when there appears to be a relatively well-run club, supporters wish to go to so much effort to play a more active role. Ultimately, the Trust's founders are inspired by the same ideals which inspired the early co-operative movement, notably self-help. The ultimate aspiration is for Celtic Football Club to be a 'club' in the true sense of the word, owned by its members, like FC Barcelona, and aspiring to the same level of footballing success. Ultimately, while the Plc vehicle might have been a useful administrative vehicle to help the club escape from the financial morass in 1995, we suspect that few Celtic fans truly believe in their heart of hearts that Celtic is a conventional business or Plc. If it is then why are there are no clamours at the AGM for a dividend, nor wholesale cashing in of shares to realize capital gains? The reason for this simple; this is an emotional investment not a financial one. Supporters want a well-managed club, but ultimately the return they most want is glory on the field. As the famous Celtic song says 'For if you know the history its enough to make your heart go...'. For those seeking financial return there are plenty of alternative investments.

Up to the time of writing, the members of the board of directors of Celtic Plc have not publicly welcomed this initiative. The Trust would like to think that their reticence reflects a well-judged caution until such time as they are in a position to judge the depth of support for the Trust concept. The Trust intends to work to ensure that strong support will indeed be forthcoming and that Celtic Plc will be willing to enter into a partnership with The Celtic Trust, and the other Celtic supporters' associations, to take the club forward.

Over the last ten months many cynics have argued that supporters are incapable of organizing themselves and that unbridled commercialization is inevitable. Our response to this is that nothing is inevitable if people decide otherwise. When BSkyB made their initial bid for Manchester United, the band of independent supporters and small supporter shareholders who opposed the bid were referred to in one magazine article as a 'ragged-arsed' collection with no hope of success. How wrong this judgement was. Through a combination of effective organization, decisive action and a passion for their club, a comparatively small group of supporters were able to galvanize opposition to the bid and ultimately stop it. Shareholders United, the Manchester United supporter-shareholder group, now has regular meetings with directors of Manchester United to discuss matters of club policy. There is no reason why Celtic supporters cannot exercise the same if not more influence at Celtic.

The contribution which the supporters make to the success of the club has long been acknowledged, although the cynical might say the fans' contribution is only praised when a financial contribution is needed. The potential contribution of fans is far greater than that. The mass of talent, experience and sheer commitment, which exists, should be harnessed for the good of Celtic. In return, the Celtic support must be given its proper place and its contribution properly acknowledged; not with flattery but with real influence and status. The great Celtic legend, Billy McNeill,[32] expresses it thus: 'Celtic are unusual among big clubs. People ask what the special Celtic feeling is all about ... It's something that grows on a player and adds an extra dimension. It's our twelfth man.' It is time for that 'extra dimension' to be felt in the boardroom as well as on the pitch.

NOTES

1. Jonathan Michie attended the first meeting of The Celtic Trust on 2 December 1999 and shared the experiences of the Manchester United supporter-shareholder organization Shareholders United of which he was a founder; Brian Lomax, founder of the pioneering Northampton Town Supporters' Trust, spoke from the platform at the first public meeting of The Celtic Trust on 5 February 2000 in Glasgow City Halls and has been a constant source of advice and strength as the Trust has taken shape; Kevin Jaquiss, from Manchester solicitors Cobbetts, played a central role in the drafting of The Celtic Trust constitution.
2. Celtic Plc, *Annual Report 1998/99*, p.2.
3. Ibid., p.32.
4. Ibid., p.11. Celtic Plc, *Annual Report 1999/2000*, p.16. In 1998–99 the club gave almost 52 per cent of pre-tax profit to charity, a total of £287,511, though this figure fell back to £10,000 in 1999/2000.
5. S. Morrow, 'If You Know the History', *Singer and Friedlander Review 1999–2000 Season* (2000), pp.22–4. S. Morrow, 'Football Clubs and the Stock Exchange: An Inappropriate Match', *Irish Accounting Review*, Vol.7, No.2 (Autumn 2000).
6. For a more detailed exposition of Celtic's history see: J.M. Bradley, *Ethnic and Religious Identity in Modern Scotland: Culture, Politics and Football* (Aldershot: Avebury, 1995); T. Campbell and P. Woods, *Dreams and Songs to Sing* (Edinburgh: Mainstream, 1999); G.P.T. Finn, 'Racism, Religion and Social Prejudice: Irish Catholic Clubs, Soccer and Scottish Society – Social Identities and Conspiracy Theories', *International Journal of the History of Sport*, Vol.8, No.3 (December 1991); B. Murray, *The Old Firm: Sectarianism, Sport and Society in Scotland* (Edinburgh: John Donald, 1984); B. Wilson, *Celtic: A Century with Honour* (London: William Collins and Sons, 1988).
7. For a more detailed exposition of the history of the Jock Stein glory years see: R. Crampsey, *Mr Stein* (Edinburgh: Mainstream, 1985); W. McNeill and A. Cameron, *Back to Paradise* (Edinburgh: Mainstream, 1988).
8. Morrow, 'Football Clubs and the Stock Exchange'.
9. Celtic Plc, *Annual Report 1998/99*, p.17.
10. *Daily Record*, 7 October 1999.
11. Morrow, 'If You Know the History'.
12. D. Conn, *The Football Business* (Edinburgh: Mainstream, 1997); S. Hamil, 'A Whole New Ball Game: Why Football Needs a Regulator', in S. Hamil, J. Michie and C. Oughton (eds.), *A Game of Two Halves? The Business of Football* (Edinburgh: Mainstream, 1999); S. Morrow, *The New Business of Football* (Basingstoke: Macmillan, 1999) Morrow, 'Football Clubs and the Stock Exchange'.
13. Hamil, 'A Whole New Ball Game: Why Football Needs a Regulator'; S. Morrow, *The New Business of Football*. Morrow, 'If You Know the History'; and Morrow, 'Football Clubs and the Stock Exchange'.
14. For a detailed exposition of the impact of increased commercialization and alleged exploitation of football fans since the early 1990s see: Conn, *The Football Business*; D. Conn, 'The New Commercialism', in Hamil *et al.*, *A Game of Two Halves?*; and Football Task Force, *Football: Commercial Issues* (London: Stationery Office, 1999).
15. Salomon Brothers, 'UK Football Clubs: Valuable Assets?', in *Global Equity Research: Leisure* (London: Salomon Brothers, 1997), pp.9–10.
16. Sir J. Smith and M. LeJeune, *Football: Its Values, Finances and Reputation* (London: The Football Association 1998), paragraph 2.8.

17. Salomon Brothers, *UK Football Clubs*, p.10.
18. Ibid.
19. J. Findlay, W.L. Holahan and C. Oughton, 'Revenue-Sharing from Broadcasting Football: The Need for League Balance', in Hamil *et al.*, *A Game of Two Halves?*.
20. 'Canned Cheering: the phantom chanter', *Financial Times*, 6 October 1999.
21. Salomon Brothers, *UK Football Clubs*.
22. For a more detailed discussion of the threat posed by media company control of football clubs see A. Brown, 'Sneaking in Through the Back Door? Media Company Interests and Dual Ownership of Clubs', in S. Hamil, J. Michie, C. Oughton and S. Warby (eds.), *Football in the Digital Age: Whose Game Is it Anyway?* (Edinburgh: Mainstream, 2000).
23. Conn, *The Football Business*; Conn, 'The New Commercialism'.
24. Morrow, 'If You Know the History'; and Morrow, 'Football Clubs and the Stock Exchange'.
25. The sub-committee consisted of HWEUCSC Club members Stephen Breen, Darren Hickey, Keith Hirstwood, Mark Sheffield, and Peter Carr along with the active encouragement of the founder member of HWEUCSC Paul Reilly.
26. Hamil *et al.*, *A Game of Two Halves?*.
27. The Co-operative Party is the political wing of the Co-operative Movement. It promotes the application of Co-operative Principles through elected representatives at all political levels, but principally through the sponsorship of candidates of the Labour Party.
28. J. Michie, *New Mutualism: A Golden Goal? Uniting Supporters and Their Clubs* (London: Co-operative Party, 1999).
29. Those in attendance were Tom Carbery, Peter Carr, Jim Devine, Jeanette Findlay, Patricia Findlay, Sean Hamil, Joe Hill, Ian McCormack, Frank McMahon, Jonathan Michie, Stephen Morrow, Jim Nelson and Christine Oughton.
30. The Celtic Supporters' Association is one of the largest, if not the largest, football club supporters' association in the UK, despite the club's poor recent results on the field. To put it in further perspective, FC Barcelona has an estimated 500 individual supporters' clubs around the world while Celtic has 400 supporters' clubs worldwide.
31. The following were elected members of the interim committee of The Celtic Trust on 20 May 2000: Chair – John McAllion MP/MSP; Vice-Chair – Alex Mosson, Lord Provost of Glasgow; Vice-Chair – Jeanette Findlay; Secretary – Peter Carr; Treasurer – Jim Devine; Sean Hamil; Joe Hill; Charles Johnston; Stephen Morrow.
32. Billy McNeill was Jock Stein's captain from 1965 through to 1974, and twice manager in 1978–83 and 1987–91.

12

Football Supporters' Relations with Their Clubs: A European Perspective

ADAM BROWN and ANDY WALSH

In the United Kingdom, a number of events and initiatives have increasingly focused attention on the role of football supporters in the governance of clubs. This is partly as a result of a politicization of football fandom over the last 15 years, which has seen a huge growth in the number and variety of fan organizations and publications.[1] The formation of the Football Supporters Association (FSA) in 1985 marked a watershed in the relations of football supporters to the running of the sport and occurred at a time of increased expression of football fan interests in the burgeoning football fanzines.[2] Underpinning this politicization has been a concern with the democratization of football motivated both by problems which football supporters have faced and the commercially-driven changes in the sport in the 1990s, in particular the formation of publicly listed holding companies owning football clubs.[3]

The campaign by Manchester United supporters against the takeover of their club by Rupert Murdoch's BSkyB TV company prompted the formation of a supporter-shareholders organization, Shareholders United, and focused attention onto mechanisms for supporter-shareholders to maximize their voting potential within clubs.[4] The experiences of supporters at lower division clubs – Northampton Town, Bournemouth, and Brighton, all of whom faced bankruptcy and expulsion from the Football League – illustrated the positive role which fans could play (in particular the formation of supporters' trusts) in both owning and running their clubs.[5] The formation of the Labour Government's Football Task Force, to investigate ways in which supporters' concerns might be met by football clubs, increased the public debate about, and scrutiny of, both football's governing bodies and the governance of football clubs.[6] The Task Force's third report, *Investing in the Community*, and in particular the recommendation that the government should help fans who wish to hold a unified stake in their club/company, led to the formation of Supporters Direct.[7]

However, increasingly elite football operates in a European, if not global, market. What then of the situation on the Continent? Has the emergence of a politicized, democratic fans' movement (however partial) been matched in other countries? Has the ownership structure of football clubs in Europe matched the changes here, in particular the flotation of clubs as public companies? And have the issues of democratization, supporter-shareholders and the governance of the sport been raised at a European level?

GENERAL DIFFERENCES

Supporters

In general terms, supporter culture in major European football nations has not changed in the way that English fan culture has. There is, for instance, no equivalent of the FSA in Germany, France, Italy or Spain. Further, although fanzines have become a feature of football life at some clubs in Germany, and *ultras* produce their own publications in Spain, they are not as numerous or as widespread as in the UK and are not a major feature of football fan culture in most other European countries. Furthermore, although some fan groups have been heavily 'political' – particularly the Italian *ultras* (see below) – generally it has been a concern with broader political issues (extreme left and right wing groupings, issues of race, nationality and regional autonomy) rather than a concern with the governance of football itself. In this scenario, football fandom becomes the site for the expression of political identities, not as a site for a political struggle itself over organization, finance and representation within football, as has happened in England.

Clubs

In England, football clubs have, since professionalization in the late nineteenth century, mainly been organized as private limited liability companies. Only in the 1990s (with one exception, Tottenham) since the Football Association's regulations on payment of directors and dividends were allowed to lapse, have clubs become publicly listed. In Continental Europe, however, football clubs have often taken the form of sporting clubs – with activities as wide as basketball, netball, and even cricket – which have either been limited companies or mutual membership organizations, or even a combination of the two.[8] Furthermore, in some countries, football associations have maintained fairly strict guidelines on public share issues and have restricted forms of ownership of football clubs.

Another key difference in the club–company organization, however, is that most Continental clubs (certainly in Spain, Italy, Germany) do not own their own grounds, which are often owned by local authorities as part of a broader local sports provision. With one or two exceptions (for example, Northampton Town in England, Borussia Dortmund in Germany), this makes the financial structure of Continental clubs – on issues of income, capital and other expenditure, liability and insurance – significantly different.

Access

Finally, one of the key issues which has prompted supporter anger in England in the 1990s has been the phenomenal increase in the cost of admission to football. It has been calculated that by 1999 the price of admission to Premier League grounds had increased by 350–400 per cent since the league's formation in 1992, prompting debate about issues of social exclusion in football.[9] Other research suggested that the increased cost was a deciding factor in the non-return of lapsed attenders at football, and as a barrier to new attenders, particularly the young.[10] However, such a situation has not been replicated on the Continent. Although the costs of salaries and transfers have increased in comparable ways to England, similarly driven by increases in broadcasting revenue streams, this has not produced similar hikes in ticket prices.

One difference is in pricing structure: whilst FC Barcelona's season tickets (excluding executive packages) range from about £50 to around £300 – a sixfold increase between the cheapest and most expensive – Manchester United's range from £323 to £456. The more segmented and 'stretched' pricing structure in some Continental clubs allows the bottom end to remain very low, maintaining access to the game. This led the Football Task Force to recommend the adoption of similar strategies in England.[11] Clearly, issues of the size of attendance, the standard and cost of living, the aforementioned form of ground ownership and the distribution of TV incomes all affect the pricing structures of clubs, but the fact remains that continental clubs have, on the whole, managed to keep prices affordable for all sections of supporters. Such disparities go some way to explaining why this issue – so potent in the United Kingdom – has not produced the kind of supporter protests and organizations which have occurred in England.

We will now consider, briefly, the relationship of fans and their organizations to club structures and the governance of the sport in three countries: Italy, Germany and Spain.

ITALY

The organizations of Italian supporters is an interesting example. Podiliri and Balestri argue that Italian ultra culture has evolved in four stages since the late 1960s.[12] Prior to 1970, they argue, political affiliations dominated Italian social life and this was reflected in support for particular teams: AC Milan for the workers and the Left, Internazionale for the bourgeoisie and the Right; the communist Emilia Romagna making Bologna's support left wing, Verona's support reflecting Veneto conservatism. The industrial unrest of 1968–69 brought new, and more extreme political formations, however, and again this impacted on football culture and supporter organization.

The first ultra groups – La Fossa dei Leoni (Lion's Den) at AC Milan, the Inter Boys, Red-Blue Commandos at Bologna – began as loose organizations creating a spectacle at Italian grounds.[13] However, as Roversi argues, although built on networks of friends and other supporters (as in other countries) 'the special feature which marked the birth of hooliganism in Italy and which was to accompany it for some time, [was that] friendship was refined in many cases by common membership of an extreme right or left-wing group... or at least of some kind of shared political experience.' Thus, 'ultra' right- or left-wing political associations began to define the ultra supporter groupings which – although there was considerable imitation of English hooligan styles at the time – marked Italian supporter organizations as distinct. This included the tightly organized structures (and on occasion violence) of extreme political organizations active at the time, the mimicking of political 'commandos' and the 'militancy, clannishness and toughness' of the organizations.

Further, these groups began to exercise a level of control over their clubs. They dominated certain sections (the curve) of the stadium which became off-limits for non-ultras. Ultras were also key players in the distribution of tickets, the production and sale of merchandise, and creating a spectacle – choreographies – in the stadium:

> The ultra group was also much more open to the outside world than other hooligan groups: because of their counter-culture tendencies, the ultra groups accepted a fairly remarkable number of women ... and carried out direct membership activities, as with political organisations. ... While English and other European supporters mainly performed spontaneous activities (such as choruses and choreographies using scarves), Italian supporters felt that the activities borrowed from politics and aimed at socialising and increasing curve support and participation were a real priority. These activities entailed an organisation that went beyond the Sunday match and involved midweek meetings where supporters worked at the creation and staging of spectacular choreographies, aimed at involving all the other *curva* supporters and at the production of various materials [e.g. merchandise] to self-finance the group.[14]

Such a level of organization and control over supporter expression, which has persisted in Italian football, is in sharp contrast to English support in the 1990s, contained in increasingly sanitized and regimented stadiums. The continuing influence of ultra groups, as well as the fact that they represent broader political and social identifications, partly explains the absence of fan organizations and publications on the English model, concerned with the political economy of football and fan representation.

Phase two of the ultra movement (1977–83) began to reflect the more violent rivalries between groups based largely on political affiliations. Violence became more highly organized, there was an increase in the use of weapons, and 'there was a greater military specialization of hooligan groups and a greater planning of clashes'.[15] Many groups began to name themselves after the political terrorist organizations of the time, brigades, and adopted left- and right-wing imagery (five pointed stars, Che Guevara, the 'New Order' axe symbol, and so on). Also, 'Directorates' – a term borrowed from far-left organizations – began to control group activity more tightly. However, their activities also 'corresponded to those typical of any organised supporters' club and were particularly devoted to organising travel to away matches, managing ticket distribution, and building a stronger relationship with team management'.[16] This relationship with the club could be very close: some ultra groups were even paid expenses by club management for their activities.[17] Such a situation – that a club's most hard core support and that which creates 'atmosphere' at grounds being paid expenses to do so – is alien to English supporter organization's experience on the whole.[18] Thus, whereas some groups in England have found it necessary to campaign for policy changes at clubs which might allow greater fan expression (the Independent Manchester United Supporters' Association's clashes with their club over standing, for example),[19] the influence exerted by, and the clubs' acceptance of, ultra organizations in Italy provides a very different context for supporter-club relations.

In the third phase of the ultras (1983–89), rivalries began to be dominated by regional affiliations as issues of local autonomy began to characterize Italian politics. There was a rise in support among northern ultra groups for organizations such as the Lombardy League and even a whole club, AC Milan, were used as a spring board to launch Silvio Berlusconi's political career with Forza Italia. The emergence of new, younger ultra groups – named after and influenced by youth and popular cultural phenomena – saw a decline in affiliation to organized politics and a reflection of the 'hedonism, exhibitionism and disaffection for political and social commitment' which dominated Italian society.[20] However, at the same time, the influx of immigrants into Italy saw increased expressions of racism among ultras which continues to this day at some clubs (e.g. Lazio).

This, and the death of Vincenzo 'Claudio' Spagnolo – a 24-year-old Genoa fan killed by Milan hooligans in 1995 – began to split some ultra groups leading to a reassessment of ultras as fan organizations. As Podaliri and Balestri write,

> recently there has been the development of a debate … on two main issues: the fact that the ultra, as football fans, are treated as second class citizens and are under strong (and frequently unjustified) pressure from public order forces; and on the other, the implications that modern football's new economic cycle has for organised supporter culture (television's immense power, the commercialisation of football, the revolutionising of football shows and the increased ticket prices are all key issues). Furthermore, some small groups and individuals are trying to develop strategies aimed at depriving racist and xenophobic groups of the control they exert.[21]

As such, we may find that the kind of concerns which in England have led to the creation of organized, cross-club fan groups concerned with the governance of the game – and to initiatives such as Supporters Direct – may also begin to emerge in Italy. Indeed, in the 1999/2000 season it was reported that the Lazio president feared to go to the Olympic Stadium in Rome, because of the reaction of Lazio ultras to the pay-per-view television deal which restricted the club's exposure.

In terms of club organization, most Italian clubs remain limited liability concerns, and some as mutual organizations. However, although Lazio and Roma are listed on the Italian *bourse*, somewhat surprisingly Berlusconi has recently ruled out the possibility of AC Milan following suit. In doing so, he hinted at the peculiar nature of football clubs as business vehicles, an argument which was put strongly in other contexts, such as England, against clubs floating: 'I'm not sure that AC Milan will float on the stock market. For me the club is not concerned with business matters. I am sceptical about football clubs going on the stock market, and I don't think it would do Milan any good.'[22] Given his previous record, his role as one of the architects of the commercial transformation of European football, and the fact that AC Milan have recently signed an extension to their lease on the San Siro stadium, such comments are surprising. However, given the experience of many English clubs – which have mostly seen their valuations slump since – Berlusconi may have learned some lessons.[23]

None of this is to say, of course, that supporters in Italy have any more control over the running of their club than their counterparts in England. It is reported that most Italian club presidents and boards maintain their position through a combination of shareholdings and systems of patronage. Thus, although Italian fans can exercise control through public pressure, especially on player issues, and although they have a distinct form of supporter organization, the issues currently being addressed in the UK over supporter shareholdings are not on the agenda in Italy.[24]

SPAIN

Historically football clubs in Spain have been organized as non-profit-making sporting clubs. The day-to-day running of the club is administered by a professional staff, with the development and direction of the club governed by a board elected by the *socios* or members. At the head of the club is an elected president whose term of office is laid down in the club statutes, or rules and regulations. As football will generally only be one part of the club, the statutes will also lay down rights of representation for each arm of the club: for example seats may be reserved on the ruling body for the basketball or handball sections.

The lack of any central regulation and the external pressures of commerce have threatened this structure so much that only four clubs out of 42 currently playing professional football in the Spanish leagues now remain as mutual sporting clubs. Clubs such as Real Madrid or Barcelona have a huge global following and are seen by business outsiders as 'brands' ripe for exploitation yet at present these two giants of the game remain in mutual ownership. One factor may be that these clubs can call on a huge following to raise finance – such as FC Barcelona's Federation scheme – or that, because of their importance, they are allowed by banks and authorities to operate with a massive debt (Real's debt was calculated at around £70m before the purchase of Luis Figo in July 2000).

There are few better examples of the depth of feeling that exists for the traditions and heritage of a football club than those witnessed at FC Barcelona.[25] Closed down twice by the military for its Catalan, as opposed to Castilian or Spanish identity, Barça is a symbol of Catalan 'national' pride: under Franco's attempts to 'unify' Spain the Nou Camp was one of the few places that Catalans could safely speak their own language. It thus holds a symbolic social, cultural and political value in its local context which is unique.

Democratic reforms in post-Franco Spain restored political rights to the Catalan people yet at FC Barcelona the democratic ideals of the past have been under attack. As Carabén *et al.* write,

> the role of the club as a shelter for the traditional Catalan values is somehow outdated. Post-Franco Spain is a democracy, Catalonia has got back in large measure its national political rights and institutions ... The problem is that in the last 20 years, under the presidency of Mr Núñez, our rights as members of the club have been dramatically reduced. In short, as Catalonians our situation has improved, but as members of Barcelona Football Club our situation has deteriorated.[26]

Josep Lluis Núñez was FC Barcelona president for 22 years during which time he systematically eroded the democracy enshrined in the club statutes. His sudden resignation at the end of the 1999/2000 season had as much to do with members' suspicions of his intentions for reforming the statutes and his attempts to further commercialize the club, as it was the performance of the team on the pitch under Louis van Gaal.

Núñez saw his commercializing proposals as 'progress' and his resignation followed the shelving of his Barça 2000 project, which would have turned the site of the Nou Camp into a theme park complete with bars, restaurants and leisure facilities. As a property developer he has made his fortune ripping down the old and replacing it with the new and he saw Barça 2000 and his constitutional reforms as a way of updating the Barça tradition. Others saw that such a project would need a great deal of external funding and, worst of all, that Barça 2000 would be the thin end of a very big wedge leading to the eventual flotation of the club. The Núñez project was stopped only after a 'shot across the bows' by way of a vote of censure against the President and his board, organized by a small but influential group of passionate *socios* called L'Elefant Blau.

Throughout Spain fans are organized into ultra groups, often producing a fanzine and organizing large, passionate, choreographed displays at matches. Barcelona has its ultra groups too, but L'Elefant Blau is unique in Spanish football.

Established in 1997 L'Elefant Blau is an association of Barça fans more akin to an independent supporters' association in England. In campaigning hard against Núñez's attempts to further undermine Barça's democracy and extend the commercialization of the club, L'Elefant Blau has proven to be a focus of opposition to many who previously felt impotent in the face of the overwhelming power and influence of Núñez. The immediate aim of the group was to stop the Barça 2000 project and then remove Núñez before going on to restore the democratic traditions on which the club had been built. The group carries the support of thousands of ordinary *socios* as well as luminaries such as the former Barcelona General Manager Armand Carabén and the charismatic ex-manager and player Johan Cruyff.

The recent election for club president saw a straight fight between Núñez's deputy president of 22 years, Joan Gaspart and Lluis Bassat, supported by L'Elefant Blau, Cruyff and others. On a 49 per cent turnout Gaspart won by 55 per cent to Bassat's 43 per cent. The number of votes cast for Bassat, whilst being a tremendous achievement for L'Elefant Blau, will also be a huge disappointment. However, the group will take consolation from the fact that their intervention and the amount of opposition to Núñez's candidate will not have pleased the Núñez camp either. Núñez spent considerable time and effort wining and dining his support among the *socios* and built a bulwark of up to 25,000 votes that saw him through his elections to office. Having failed again to lift the vote much above this loyalist threshold, the Núñez camp will still be looking over their shoulders at the gathering forces around L'Elefant Blau which will help to keep the commercial bandwagon in the lay-by for a little while yet. Gaspart's comment on gaining office that he wished to re-unite the club was tantamount to acknowledging that Núñez had done much to divide it and he invited Bassat to work with the new board and president. The next five years will see L'Elefant Blau continue to campaign for greater democracy within FC Barcelona and Núñez's demise will act as a reminder to Gaspart that the club belongs to all its members not to a ruling elite.

The election of Florentino Perez against expected victor and incumbent Lorenzo Sanz as Real Madrid's President sent another shock wave through Spanish football. Although that campaign was dominated by the pre-election promises of the candidates as to which one would sign which player (Perez famously promised either he would buy Luis Figo, or he would pay for the season tickets of all members and ended up with the more expensive option of Figo!), and was less concerned with the organization of the club and the role of supporters within it, the maintenance of a mutual structure at the two giants of Spanish football provides an interesting contrast to the corporate governance structures increasingly dominating the English game at the elite level.

GERMANY

There has been little opposition from supporters' groups to the creeping commercialization of football in Germany. This may be more to do with the fact that clubs have been careful not to alienate fans with hefty price increases than anything else, but there is a more cautious approach to the business development of the modern game in Germany than has been witnessed in England. The German Football Association (DFB) has done much more than its English counterpart to preserve traditional club structures and many fans have a faith in the governors of German football to administer the game which would make the Football Association (FA) in Lancaster Gate as green as the Wembley pitch.

To participate in the Bundesliga each club has to apply for a licence every year from the German FA and until as recently as October 1998 the statutes of the German FA only allowed the granting of licences to clubs constituted as sporting clubs. Attempts were made by SV Hamburg in 1991 and Werder Bremen in 1992 to become joint-stock companies but this was disallowed as it would be against Bundesliga rules so the proposals never went ahead.

Ironically, at a time when the chairmen of English clubs are telling fans that their clubs need to float to keep up with Continental rivals, the Germans (as with some Italian clubs) look upon what has happened in England with some scepticism and the experience of English clubs floating on the stock exchange has instilled a sense of caution in the minds of those administering the game in Germany. Changes to regulations brought about in 1999, however, do allow flotations although crucially the regulations stipulate that if a club does decide to float then 50 per cent of the shares, plus one share, must remain in the hands of the parent sporting club, or *mutterverein*. This rule is designed to protect the interests of the club members, preventing any asset stripping of the resources built up through the years of mutual ownership. The fear that the bigger clubs such as Borussia Dortmund and Bayern Munich could leave the rest of the Bundesliga behind in financial terms if they decided to float has led to the idea of a 'solidarity fund' being proposed. The idea has only been raised tentatively so far but each club would have to pay into the fund dependent on its relative wealth so that the poorer clubs could be supported. Such a situation contrasts sharply with the English experience where the FA allowed its own rules on ownership – such as restrictions on dividend payments and payments to directors – to be circumvented without any conditions to protect the future health of the whole game at all.

It was always believed that there would be a race to the stock market led by Bayern Munich and Borussia Dortmund, but Bayern Munich's General Manager, Uli Hoeness, has declared that Bayern will not be floating as the club is doing quite well as it is currently constituted. At Dortmund only four members voted against the club being floated with 1,200 voting in favour, though the vote has not yet been acted upon. The reaction from the fans has been that when things have not been going too well on the pitch they have taken it out on the players more vociferously than they may have done in the past. With the huge rise in wages it is the players who are seen as the major beneficiaries of the proposed reforms. The club hierarchies have been less criticized.

Some other clubs are moving towards trading on the stock market: Borussia Mochengladbach is a fully constituted Plc or AG (*Aktiengesellschaft*), but its shares are not being traded on the market at the time of writing as the commercial conditions are not considered favourable, due to uncertainty and a lack of sporting success. Clubs do also have the option to become private limited companies (Gesellschaft mit beschränkter Haftung), or GmbH, as is the case at Wolfsburg and Bayer Leverkusen. Wolfsburg is 80%-owned by the VW motor company, which has its headquarters in the town. Likewise, Bayer 04 Leverkusen are 80% owned by the Bayer corporation. Ironically, both companies own a stake that it is higher than the 49.9% which is allowed by the DfB statutes under a special clause which states that corporations that have substantially funded clubs for at least 20 years will be exempted from the 49% rule.

Hertha Berlin – who stated their intentions to go public in the summer of 1999 but neither as a GmbH or as an AG – chose instead a formulation recommended by the German FA which is a crossover between a partnership and a publicly quoted company, Kommanditgesellschaft auf Aktien or KgaA. Under this model the German FA recommends that the *mutterverein* retain 75 per cent of the stock thus preventing a complete takeover of the club. A three-quarters majority is seen as sufficient to protect the interests of the members as this would usually be enough to make any major changes to the company constitution. Additionally, as the shares carry no voting rights, there is little threat to the interests of the *Mutterverein*. Furthermore, at some clubs a supervisory board operates which oversees the operations of both commercial and sporting sides of the club, although often without much power.

The effect of these restrictions may have put off potential investors from actually taking clubs over but adversity is the mother of invention and has led to other deals being done. Borussia Dortmund decided to float the club's merchandising operation at the end of 1999, which may lead to an increase in the number of luminous yellow Dortmund shirts found across Europe!

In terms of fans' influence in German clubs, in these confusing times, different formulations of ownership produce a very varied picture. Whereas fans at Frankfurt have found their influence declining – before the Octagon deal and rule changes they could elect the president of the club every two years – at Hamburg SV supporters have reacted to the changes elsewhere by reaffirming their role in the club structure, with 18,000 club members and 11,000 members of the supporters' club. Further, at clubs such as Schalke 04 and St Pauli, large left-wing supporter followings have found expression, challenging the commercial direction of the German game's development, as well as the rise of fascist supporter groups, particularly in the East.[27] Even at the more successful, commercially driven clubs such as Dortmund, the management have managed to remain relatively popular because 'its policies appear modest and considerate; the club continuously celebrates its working class traditions and emphasizes its obligations to its local community'.[28]

However, as has happened earlier in England, television income is transforming the landscape. The bidding process for the rights to broadcast games on TV is as fiercely competitive in Germany as it is elsewhere in the world and clubs will readily look to this as an area to maximize investment from outside. During the bidding for the rights to broadcast Bundesliga 1 and Bundesliga 2 games on TV, Dortmund voted at a meeting of the Bundesliga clubs against the central marketing of TV rights. The DFB voted for the eventual deal with ISPR, whose chief rivals in the bidding war was UFA Sports GmbH, a Hamburg-based company owned by CTL-UFA of Luxembourg. Dortmund wanted clubs to be able to negotiate the rights to televise their matches themselves, and has since sold some TV and marketing rights to UFA for 50 million Deutschmarks. Clubs at the bottom of the league will thus still get a share of the TV money, although their slice of the cake has been cut, and they will no longer get a share of the monies paid for Champions League and UEFA Cup games, as was the case in the past.

CTL-UFA declares that it is Europe's biggest company in the field of 'Electronics Leisure', owning 40 TV and radio stations across the Continent. UFA claims tie-ins at over 250 football clubs plus 50 national teams and as such is a major player in European football. To break into the German football TV market UFA has been buying the marketing rights at a number of clubs. The best bargains and most attractive are clubs who have had an illustrious past but have since fallen on hard times. Desperate to climb back up the pile and regain some of their past glory, UFA's approaches have been welcomed by fans and club officials alike. Other companies with a similar approach are Kinowelt AG, which is keen to screen matches in local cinemas, and Sportwelt, which has an interest in up to a dozen clubs including Fortuna Düssledorf.

The sale of marketing and TV rights to large outside companies for fixed term contracts appears to be a sensible way of raising finance, because clubs retain their long-term ownership of the rights themselves whilst gaining expert assistance in how best to handle what is an extremely complex business. However, as the stakes rise, TV companies may begin, as in England, to demand a greater say in the structure of the club, including holding minority stakes.[29] Also, however welcome this new revenue stream is, as with other European countries, increased TV revenues have not offset increases in expenditure: whilst income has increased by 180 per cent since 1990, expenditure has gone up by around 280 per cent.[30] It is also estimated that German clubs have a collective debt of £200m and pressure may soon come to bear on the low entrance cost of German football.

The question remains, however, of how long the Bundesliga and DFB can retain their control over the ownership structure of its biggest clubs, before the draw of the G14 group starts to pull the likes of Bayern Munich and Borussia Dortmund towards a European breakaway league. The 1999 Media Partners proposals[31] for an expanded Champions League format was championed by the likes of Karl-Heinz Rummenigge and, although the immediate threat may have ebbed, like the ocean's tide, it will return and questions remain about whether the defences are strong enough to resist it next time. The clubs run the risk of becoming dependent on the companies that purchase their marketing and TV rights. UFA have already tried to force out the boss of Hamburger SV, Werner Hackmann, even going to the lengths of hiring 22 phoney club members and an actor for 500 marks a head in a bid to prevent his election at the AGM. Hackmann sits on the Bundesliga Committee at the DFB, the German FA. There, although he has done nothing to oppose UFA, he has not done anything to help them either. So UFA tried to get rid of him. The DFB has now ruled that company representatives may not sit on boards at more than one club. UFA, for example, had people on the Supervisory Boards at both Hamburg and Hertha Berlin. Clubs in breach of this rule will be refused a licence. This has been done to stop clubs exerting undue influence on the affairs of different clubs playing in the same league, with all the obvious implications.

Whilst the German model may appear preferable to supporters of clubs which are Plcs in England, the sort of money now on offer to Europe's elite clubs could eventually see all the efforts of the German FA cast aside in a trice. The response of the German fans and their organizations will be one to watch.

CONCLUSIONS

The varied traditions, organization and finance of both football clubs and supporter organizations in Europe make simple comparisons with the UK difficult. In this sense, Tomlinson and Sugden are correct to argue that 'Football is a cultural product, and its meanings and significance are not wholly defined by its political economy. People in pubs or domestic lounges, as well as at live games ... negotiate the expression of a particular cultural identity through the public culture of the game.'[32] However, as they go on, it is also correct to say that 'at the top level, football represents more and more graphically the triumph of the universal market and whenever it is watched ... it is an increasingly commodified cultural product in a structured environment of an intensifyingly exclusive type'. The globalization of football, therefore, and the free market context in which it operates, is beginning to put familiar pressures on the organization and finance of clubs and leagues, and nowhere is this more true than in Europe. Thus, despite their unique histories and distinct national and local contexts, we are beginning to see similar processes and developments in the major European leagues to those in the UK.

The implementation of the *Bosman* ruling, the increased integration of media and sport companies, increases in expenditure, and increased pressures on clubs to maximize income streams are beginning to raise the same issues and concerns among supporters as we have seen in the UK. The emergence of supporter groups such as L'Elefant Blau at Barcelona and Club NR12 at Bayern Munich and the transnational co-operation between such fans groups suggest that similar pressures to those which produced a politicization of supporter organizations in England may happen increasingly across the Continent.[33] Indeed, the issue of supporter involvement in owning and controlling clubs is itself already emerging, although in a context in which fans have traditionally had a greater role in club policy than in the UK.

Finally, another issue which will be important is the role of the European Commission. Increasingly the place of sport, and football in particular, within Europe is an issue of concern, both to competition authorities and to the Education and Culture Directorate.[34] The importance the Commission places on maintaining sport's social function in an increasingly mediatized and commercialized context may have major implications for the game's governance and will certainly affect the relationships of European fans to their clubs.

NOTES

The authors would like to thank Stuart Dykes for his invaluable help and comments. For further analysis of recent trends in German football see S. Dykes, 'Commercialisation and Fan Participation in Germany', in S. Hamil, J. Michie, C. Oughton and S. Warby (eds.), *Football in the Digital Age: Whose Game Is it Anyway?* (Edinburgh: Mainstream, 2000).

1. A. Brown, 'Lets All have a Disco? Football, Popular Music and Democratisation', in J. O'Connor, S. Redhead and D. Wynne (eds.), *The Clubcultures Reader* (Oxford: Blackwell, 1997). A. Brown, 'United We Stand: Problems with Fan Democracy', in A. Brown (ed.), *Fanatics! Power, Identity and Fandom in Football* (London: Routledge, 1998).
2. T. Burke, J. Horne and D. Jary, 'Football Fanzines and Football Culture: A Case of Successful Cultural Contestation?', *Sociology*, Special Edition, Vol.39, No.3 (August 1991). R. Haynes, *The Football Imagination* (Aldershot: Avebury, 1995).
3. R. Taylor, *Football and Its Fans: Supporters and Their Relation to the Game: 1885-1985* (Leicester: Leicester University Press, 1992). D. Conn, *The Football Business* (Edinburgh: Mainstream, 1997).
4. A. Brown and A. Walsh, *Not For Sale! Manchester United, Murdoch and the Defeat of BSkyB* (Edinburgh: Mainstream, 1999).
5. B. Lomax, 'Fan Representation on the Board: The Case of Northampton Town FC', in S. Hamil, J. Michie and C. Oughton (eds.), *A Game of Two Halves? The Business of Football* (Edinburgh: Mainstream, 1999). T. Watkins, *Cherries in the Red: How One Football Fan Saved His Club and Became Chairman* (London: Headline, 1998).
6. A. Brown, 'Thinking the Unthinkable or Playing the Game? New Labour, the Football Task Force and the Reform of English Football', in Hamil *et al.*, *A Game of Two Halves?*. A. Brown, 'The Football Task Force and the Regulator Debate', in S. Hamil, J. Michie, C. Oughton and S.Warby (eds.), *Football in the Digital Age: Whose Game Is it Anyway?* (Edinburgh: Mainstream, 2000). A. Brown, 'Taken to Task: the Football Task Force, Government and Regulating the People's Game', in S. Greenfield and G. Osborn, *Law and Sport in Contemporary Society* (London and Portland, OR: Frank Cass, 2000).
7. Football Task Force, *Investing in the Community* (London: Stationery Office, 1999).
8. J. Burns, *Barça: A People's Passion* (Edinburgh: Mainstream, 1999). P. Lanfranchi, 'Exporting Football: Notes on the Development of Football in Europe', in R. Giulianotti and J. Williams (eds.), *Game Without Frontiers: Football, Identity and Modernity* (Aldershot: Avebury, 1994).
9. Football Task Force, *Football: Commercial Issues* (London: Stationery Office, 1999).
10. S. Perkins and J. Williams, *Ticket Pricing, Football Business and 'Excluded' Football Fans* (Leicester: Leicester University Press, 1999).
11. Football Task Force, *Football: Commercial Issues*.
12. C. Podiliri and C. Balestri, 'The Ultras, Racism and Football Culture in Italy', in A. Brown (ed.), *Fanatics! Power, Identity and Fandom in Football* (London: Routledge, 1998).

13. A. Roversi, 'The Birth of the "Ultras": The Rise of Football Hooliganism in Italy', in R. Giulianotti and J. Williams (eds.), *Game Without Frontiers: Football, Identity and Modernity* (Aldershot: Avebury, 1994).

14. Podiliri and Balestri, 'The Ultras, Racism and Football Culture in Italy', p.91.

15. Ibid., p.92.

16. Ibid., p.93.

17. Ibid., p.94.

18. Taylor, *Football and Its Fans*.

19. S. Lee, 'From Grey Shirts to Grey Suits: The Political Economy of English Football in the 1990s', in A. Brown (ed.), *Fanatics! Power, Identity and Fandom in Football* (London: Routledge, 1998); Brown, 'United We Stand'.

20. Podiliri and Balestri, 'The Ultras, Racism and Football Culture in Italy', p.95.

21. Ibid., p.99.

22. eurosoccer.com, 15 July 2000.

23. Football Task Force, *Football: Commercial Issues*.

24. A. Roversi, *The Rich and the Poor in Italian Football*, in S. Redhead (ed.), *The Passion and the Fashion: Football Fandom in the New Europe* (Aldershot: Avebury, 1992).

25. Burns, *Barça: A People's Passion*. A. Carabén, A. Godall and J. Laporta, 'The Struggle for Democracy at FC Barcelona and the case for a European independent regulator of professional football', in Hamil *et al.*, *Football in the Digital Age*.

26. A. Carabén, A. Godall, J. Laporta and J. Moix, 'The Struggle for Democracy at Barcelona FC', in Hamil *et al.*, *A Game of Two Halves?*.

27. U. Merkel, 'Football Identity and Youth Culture in Germany', in G. Armstrong and R. Giulianotti (eds.), *Football Cultures and Identities* (London: Macmillan, 1999).

28. Ibid., p.54.

29. A. Brown, 'Sneaking in Through the Back Door? Media Company Interests and Dual Ownership of Clubs', in Hamil *et al.*, *Football in the Digital Age*.

30. Merkel, 'Football Identity and Youth Culture in Germany', p.55.

31. See A. Bell, 'Sport and the Law: The Influence of European Union Competition Policy on the Traditional League Structures of European Football', in Hamil *et al.* (eds.), *Football in the Digital Age*, p.126.

32. J. Sugden and A. Tomlinson, *FIFA and the Contest for World Football* (Cambridge: Polity Press, 1998), p.98.

33. Brown and Walsh, *Not For Sale!*, Ch.5.

34. A. Brown, 'European Football and the European Union: Governance, Participation and Social Cohesion – Towards a Research Policy Agenda, *Soccer and Society*, Vol.1, No.2 (Summer 2000).

13

How Democracy Saved Northampton Town FC

BRIAN LOMAX

The relationship between the football industry, football clubs and supporters is complex. Although the contemporary football industry has become big business, and many clubs are placing marketing activities at the top of their agendas, it is too simplistic to view fans in terms of merely being 'customers' of the game. Their commitment normally extends to investing a degree of time, energy and loyalty, as well as money, into the club they support. The essence of the 'customer' relationship – that a person makes a rational choice in the market place by selecting a product that he or she considers the best value for money – is largely absent from the relationship between the fan and the club he or she supports. Most football supporters 'choose' their club at a young age, and then stick to this choice, however irrational it may seem at face value. Even if the team is struggling, and the 'product' could be seen to be substandard, many supporters continue to invest in their chosen club. These fans view their club differently from how they may regard other leisure services or retail outlets, and feel a type of emotional bond that does not exist in these other spheres. Yet this bond, powerful as it is, can leave supporters open to exploitation by football clubs, which may overcharge for replica team kits or tickets, for example.

In order to prevent this kind of exploitation, and to give supporters a genuine voice and a sense of empowerment, a number of fan groups have appeared since the mid-1980s.[1] The national Football Supporters Association gained a high profile during this time, and successfully campaigned on a number of issues, including the prevention of the identity card scheme for supporters, an idea proposed in the late 1980s by the then Prime Minister Margaret Thatcher. Other fans' groups have also appeared, including a plethora of independent supporters' associations, and those campaigning on single issues, such as opposing racism.[2] Yet fans have very rarely achieved tangible power *within* a football club, and particularly in the boardroom. The first club successfully to integrate a supporter onto the club's board of directors was the one I support, Northampton Town, and this essay will outline the history and benefits of this development. Through forming a supporters' trust, fans at the club have managed to obtain a seat on the board of directors, and the trust would strongly recommend that every football club should have elected supporter representation on the board of directors. Not only is it morally right, it also works; but in order to be effective the process of electing a fan must be truly democratic and involve a degree of accountability, and I shall discuss these points in more detail at the end of this piece.

Within the context of supporter empowerment, I wish specifically to address the first three items of the Football Task Force's 'Terms of Reference': anti-racism, access for disabled supporters and greater supporter involvement in the running of clubs. At least in the case of Northampton Town, these three issues are organically linked and interconnected. In order to establish this case, a brief introductory explanation of the origins and role of the Northampton Town Supporters' Trust is necessary.

NORTHAMPTON TOWN SUPPORTERS' TRUST: A BRIEF HISTORY

Northampton Town Supporters' Trust was formed in January 1992, as a result of a large public meeting attended by over 600 fans. This meeting was called by a group of ordinary supporters, including Rob Marshall, editor of the fanzine *What a Load of Cobblers*, and myself, in response to a financial crisis at the club and a series of misleading statements issued by the then chairman. The club was reluctant to send representatives to the meeting, but relented at the last minute, and the situation disclosed by them was a debt approaching £1.6 million, representing more than two years' turnover for the club. As the Trust subsequently discovered, the rot had set in some time before, and unpaid bills stretched back several years, to the time of the previous régime at the club. The crisis, however, had been precipitated by the club's failure to pay the previous two months' players' wages, which amounted to about £64,000. The Professional Footballers' Association had had to cover this, and so it too had now become a creditor of the club.

The Trust was set up with two objectives: first, to raise money to save the club (but not for the incumbent régime), and to be accountable to the supporters for the expenditure of that money; and second, to seek effective involvement and representation for supporters in the running of the club in order to ensure that such a crisis situation would never occur again. In this latter respect, the Trust marked itself out as being distinct from normal supporters' clubs, in that from its inception it has had an inescapably political dimension. By doing this, the Trust was a forerunner of a variety of independent supporters' associations and other similar bodies, who have sought to change the way that their clubs are run and how they relate to their fans.[3] The Trust has also had a representative of Northampton Borough Council on its executive committee since its inception.

The Trust's initial strategy was a dual approach: campaigning for change and fundraising in public, whilst negotiating in private with the club's creditors, former directors, the Football League and the Professional Footballers' Association. In this way the Trust was able to establish its credentials within the first three months to play its part in the running of the club.

The Trust's publicity campaign met with almost universal support from the public and the media. Fundraising efforts began spontaneously in pubs, clubs and workplaces, and dozens of individual donations ranging from £1 to £1,000 were received. A bucket collection at the first home match after the Trust was formed yielded £3,500, over £1 per head of the gate. This particular occasion became immortalized locally by the chairman's attempts to evict the collectors from the ground in front of television cameras. In the eyes of supporters, this only added to the legitimacy of the Trust and its members, and the bucket collections continued successfully for the rest of the season.

The private negotiations were aimed at bringing a winding-up petition against the club in court. Strange though it may seem that loyal supporters might take such drastic action, the advice we received was that this was the only way to wrest control from the chairman. The Trust could not, of course, bring the petition itself, because it was not a creditor of the club, so we had to persuade others to take this course. The company that eventually did so was Abbeyfield Press Limited, the club programme's producers, who were owed over £11,000. Abbeyfield was owned by Tim Vernon, himself a lifelong supporter, and his partner. Despite pressure from various quarters, they stood firm and went ahead with the action.

When the petition was brought, the chairman was granted an eight-week adjournment on the basis of preparing a 'rescue plan' for the club. This was worrying because it would have taken until the end of the season when, with fixtures completed, the Football League would have had much less incentive to help keep the club going. For a brief period it appeared that the club's only future lay in the route already taken by Aldershot Football Club, which found that after the old company folded in 1992 and a new one formed, the team itself had to resume playing five divisions lower in the league 'pyramid'. Northampton Town's only 'assets' in these circumstances would have been the £13,000 thus far raised by the Trust, and the right to continue playing at the old County Ground. This ground no longer even met Southern League Premier Division standards.

The chairman's 'rescue plan' collapsed within days and shortly afterwards he called in administrators to run the club. On his own admission, he thought that by doing this he would obtain a year's breathing space, and then return to run a club free of debt. Barry Ward, the administrator, took a different view. He first had to obtain an Order of Administration from the High Court and in order to do so had to convince the Court that the company was capable of returning to solvency and normal trading within a reasonable period of time. His two main pieces of evidence were the continued interest of former directors, and the volume of public support as evidenced by the formation and rapid growth of the Trust. The Trust, meanwhile, was continuing its public work through fundraising, bucket collections and open meetings.

On obtaining the Order of Administration, Ward's first action was to cancel the contracts of the three management staff and nine players. This led to much sorrow and heart-searching among supporters, but they fundamentally knew some sort of action of this kind was necessary to bring costs under control. The process of political education had already begun.

The same morning, Ward held a meeting at his offices in Birmingham to which former directors and Trust officers were invited. The chairman and his wife were already present when Phil Frost, another Trust officer, and myself arrived. Barry told us all that he was forming a local board to run the club on his behalf, of which he would be chairman. He then invited us to decide whether the current chairman and his wife – by then the sole directors – would continue in post, and left us to discuss the matter. We took the opportunity to vote them out, and at that point they left with good grace. The meeting then resumed and it was agreed that the new board would consist of four former directors and two representatives of the Trust. We insisted that they be elected. On 10 April 1992 Phil Frost and I became the first two elected supporters' directors on the board of an English League club.

When the club came out of administration and returned to normal trading in 1994, this was reduced to one but that place is guaranteed by Northampton Borough Council until at least the year 2019 as a condition of the club's lease and licence to occupy its new stadium at Sixfields, Northampton, which was completed in 1994. The Borough Council also has a non-executive seat on the board for the same duration.

This stadium, built and owned by Northampton Borough Council with the aid of a £1 million grant from the Football Trust, is a perfect symbol of the partnership between the local authority, the football club and the Trust. It is also state-of-the-art in its safety provisions and its facilities for disabled spectators. It is truly a community stadium. The Leader of the Council has recently said that he regards the Trust member on the board of directors as representing not only the supporters but the community as a whole. Councillors have also frequently stated that the stadium would never have been built were it not for the Supporters' Trust and the democratic guarantee it provided. If the Trust had not existed it would have been politically unacceptable to provide a football ground from public funds for an unreformed club recently guilty of gross mismanagement.

In financial terms, the Trust has paid over £105,000 into Northampton Town FC in the last seven years, with funds still in hand, and it owns 31,592 shares in the club, over seven per cent of the total issued. The sum invested bears good comparison with that of any individual director over the same period.

We have advised or assisted in the formation of several Trusts at other clubs, with similar objectives, at Kettering Town, Middlesbrough, Plymouth Argyle and AFC Bournemouth. These trusts have enjoyed varying degrees of success, the most notable being AFC Bournemouth, to which I will refer later. We have also advised groups who wish to form similar trusts at Dundee United, Manchester City, Partick Thistle, Lincoln City and Chester City among others.

I now turn to the Task Force Terms of Reference, with the assertion that certain key developments at the football club have stemmed entirely from the Trust's representation on the board and the three-way partnership with the Council described above.

THE ELIMINATION OF RACISM

In November 1995 a working party was set up at Northampton Town to organize the relaunch of the 'Let's Kick Racism Out Of Football' campaign at local level. I was asked to chair this working party, which now has representatives from the Supporters' Trust, the football club, Northampton Borough Council, Baxter and Platt Ltd (the Sixfields Stadium Management Company), the Commission for Racial Equality, Northampton Racial Equality Council, Northamptonshire Police, the Scarman Centre at the University of Leicester, Middlesex University, the British Asian Association, Northamptonshire County Council, the 'Kick It Out' campaign, Northampton Town Football in the Community, and Nationwide Building Society. After successfully achieving the initial objective of bringing the aims and message of the campaign to the supporters' attention, at the home match against Darlington in February 1996, we decided that this one-off gesture was insufficient, and therefore set ourselves the task of drafting an equal opportunities policy for the football club. The working party examined various examples, and chose to base the policy upon that used by the charity of which I am chief executive, but adapted to meet the particular needs and circumstances of a football club. It was adopted unanimously by the board of directors in October 1996, and then in public on the pitch at our home match against Chester in January 1997, in the presence of Members of Parliament and other distinguished guests.

Thus Northampton Town became the first League football club formally to have adopted an equal opportunities policy. Since then, the club has been contacted by others who wish to do the same, many of whom have been referred to the club by the Football League or the Football Association. The policy has already had a number of positive outcomes in terms of anti-racist education of supporters, who will now habitually report and identify offenders within the crowd. The board has approved a banning policy for those established as guilty of racist words or behaviour.

This match was designated the Walter Tull Memorial Match, in honour of the club's first black player. Walter was only the second black professional footballer in history.[4] He joined Northampton Town from Tottenham Hotspur in 1911, and played over 100 games for the Cobblers, scoring nine goals from midfield. In 1914 he was among the initial army volunteers at the outbreak of the First World War, and two years later became the first black officer to receive a commission in the British Army. He was killed in action in 1918 on the Somme, only weeks before the Armistice, and has no known grave. In partnership with the Borough Council, the working party has now established a Walter Tull Memorial Garden at Sixfields, where the ashes of those supporters who request it may be interred. This was officially dedicated in July 1999.

Northampton Town 'Football in the Community', of which I was also chair, recently launched a highly successful initiative to establish regular 'Football Fun Days' for the Bangladeshi youth in the town, in collaboration with the local Mosque and Muslim Community Centre. It is believed that this is another 'first' for Northampton Town, reaching out to a community who for various reasons have had little contact with local football, although they love the game.

IMPROVING DISABLED ACCESS

Northampton Town have been pioneers in addressing the issue of playing opportunities for people with disabilities. The 'Football in the Community Scheme' has taken the lead in organizing league football on a national level for players with learning disabilities, so much so that when the England learning disabilities team won the European Cup in Belgium in 1996 (beating Germany 4–2), eight of the squad and the team manager were from Northampton Town. The club has also been in the forefront of establishing the first Duke of Edinburgh's Award Centre with specific emphasis on disabled candidates, at Sixfields in 1997. In 1998 the club hosted two of the quarter-finals of the World Cup for players with learning disabilities.

In terms of spectator facilities, in 1997 Northampton Town won the Football League Award and the overall McDonald's Award (England, Scotland and Wales) for the best disabled spectator facilities in British football. Sixfields is the only football ground in the country to allocate over one per cent of its entire capacity to disabled spectators and, at the time of writing, is the only ground with dedicated disabled areas on all four sides, thus giving the maximum choice of where and with whom disabled fans wish to watch the match. Whilst the major credit for this must go to Northampton Borough Council, who built the stadium, the award was not only for physical facilities but for customer services. The Supporters' Trust, too, has played its part. Since its inception in 1992, it has generated several thousands of pounds for the better provision of facilities for disabled fans through an annual fundraising event, this money most recently being used for the purchase of Sennheisser Units to relay a match commentary within the stadium to supporters with sight problems.

SUPPORTER INVOLVEMENT IN THE RUNNING OF CLUBS

Northampton Town Supporters' Trust organizes regular monthly open forums for all supporters, whether Trust members or not. Speakers have included the chairman and directors of the football club, the manager, the secretary, members of the playing staff, the local police and the stadium management company. At all meetings the elected director is present and available to answer any questions about the running of the club. Many policies have been changed or improved as a result of discussions at these meetings, including, for example, the thorny issue of ticket pricing.

The elected director is subject to annual re-election by single transferable vote, and must therefore remain active and sensitive to the views of the membership if he or she is to retain the position. The chairman in the 1999/2000 season was local Member of Parliament Tony Clarke. After seven years the Trust's membership now stands at a record level, as do attendances at its meetings which average over 100.

In the time since the Trust joined the board of directors, average attendances have risen from 2,000 to over 6,000. This growth in support is, of course, related to the team's success and the new stadium, but it is interesting to note that the gates had already risen to over 3,500 before the club went to Sixfields in October 1994, and while the team was still near the bottom of Division Three. The increase is, in my view, partly because supporters now know they are stakeholders and not just turnstile fodder. Price increases for tickets have been accepted because they have been properly explained and justified, and not just imposed 'from above'. There is a feeling of everyone being on the same side in a common enterprise, rather than the supporters developing an 'us and them' mentality in their relationship with the club. That is not to say that there are not disagreements and tensions – there are – but there is a forum for resolving them and arriving at acceptable solutions. The club's historic debt has now been paid off in its entirety, the last payment of £50,000 having been made in August 1998.

The involvement of supporters at director level has therefore produced commercial as well as social advantages for the football club. The chief benefits, I believe, have been felt in the areas identified above: anti-racism, equal opportunities and disability, on which the voice of the Trust has been specific and radical. In these areas it is delivering the policies and services of the local authority in a very high-profile context, and thus is a truly equal partner with them. The club is also succeeding where other boards of directors, who often do not prioritize issues such as racism or disability, fail to act.

Historically, it has usually taken a crisis such as potential insolvency before directors have turned to supporters for help and participation. There is no good reason why this should be so, given the number of successful outcomes we have witnessed from fan involvement at Northampton which were unrelated to the club's financial position. Northampton Town is living proof that supporters' democracy, and close attention to social issues, do not preclude success on the pitch: two Wembley play-offs in successive seasons and promotion tell their own story! Although the club was unfortunately relegated back to Division Three in 1998/99, the infrastructure in place ensured that the organization continued to be run competently and solvently. The point was proved when we were promoted back to Division Two 12 months later.

CONCLUSIONS

Over the last seven years, and particularly recently, I have been contacted by officials and/or supporters of nearly 50 clubs, who either wish to form a Trust similar to our own, or to achieve democratic supporter representation on their board of directors, or both. As a result of detailed discussions with all these people, I believe that in order to be effective on any lasting basis, a scheme for supporter representation on the board must have five hallmarks.

First, the scheme should ensure that any supporter elected to the board enjoys full *executive* powers, rather than merely non-voting or purely observer status, as has been tried elsewhere. The directorship must be registered as such at Companies House, and carry with it the entitlement to full access to all board meetings in their entirety, and to all written and financial information available to the other directors. Symbolic or bogus experiments like the one by Francis Lee at Manchester City expose the limitations of anything less.

Second, the scheme must be truly *democratic*, ensuring one person one vote, not one pound one vote. A bond scheme such as was launched at Charlton Athletic entitling subscribers to a vote for each unit purchased, to elect a director, is not democratic, and in fact merely enshrines the concept that money speaks louder than supporters in football.

Third, and following on from the above point, it must be *affordable* for all supporters. If a subscription is the basis of the electorate, it must not be set at a level which is beyond the purse of any supporter, despite the temptation to use subscriptions as a quick fundraiser. The Supporters' Trust at Northampton has subscription levels at £5 per year for adults, £2 per year for 'concessions' (old and young), and £25 for life. These rates have not been increased since our formation.

Fourth, the scheme must be *entrenched*, so that it cannot be set aside at the whim of the board if the representative says or does something the other directors do not like, or fails to come up with a sum of money requested. As previously stated, the Trust at Northampton is fortunate to have its position guaranteed in the stadium lease until 2019 at least. Similar opportunities arise wherever clubs become involved in partnerships with their local authority, whether over the stadium or some other financial contract or arrangement. The sad example of Kettering Town, where the Trust representative was cast aside by the new owners following a short period of administration, illustrates the importance of this point.

Last, the scheme must be *independent*, meaning that the representative, and the Trust where applicable, retain the right to criticize the club and the board on behalf of supporters when all other avenues have failed. This, it appears to me, is the snag with the otherwise highly successful example of AFC Bournemouth, where a Trust, initiated by key supporters but comprising a coalition of local interests, acquired the football club two years ago. When the honeymoon period ends, as inevitably one day it will, who will the supporters criticize? Themselves?

And who will be in a position to represent them in doing so? Also, I am not aware of any democratic structures having been put in place there during the last two years to enable supporters to decide who they want to represent them in future.

Lastly, we at Northampton have been greatly encouraged by the endorsement we have received from the Football Task Force in all the reports which they have published, most notably the third, 'Investing in the Community'; and the fourth on 'Commercial Issues'.[5] These reports give approval to the twin principles of democratic supporters' trusts, and of elected supporter representation on boards of directors. With the help of Supporters Direct[6] I hope this proves to be a prelude to a period when full supporter involvement is the rule rather than the exception.[7]

NOTES

This essay is an updated version of an article of the same name which first appeared in the journal *Soccer & Society*: B. Lomax, 'The Future of Football: Challenges for the Twenty-First Century', *Soccer and Society*, 1, 1 (Spring 2000), 79–87. The amendments bring the story of the Northampton Town Supporters' Trust up to date. The piece has been substantially reproduced here because the story of the formation of the Northampton Town Supporters' Trust is central to the development of the supporters trust movement in Britain. A full understanding of the supporters' trust phenomena requires an understanding of the events at Northampton.

1. For analyses of the relationship between clubs and supporters, see, for example, S. Redhead, *Post Fandom and the Millennial Blues: The Transformation of Soccer Culture* (London: Routledge, 1997); R. Taylor, *Football and its Fans: Supporters and Their Relations with the Game, 1885–1985* (Leicester: Leicester University Press, 1992); and A. Brown (ed.), *Fanatics! Power, Identity and Fandom in Football* (London: Routledge, 1998).
2. An examination of the efficacy of antiracist fan groups can be found in J. Garland and M. Rowe, 'Field of Dreams: An Assessment of Antiracism in British Football', *Journal of Ethnic and Migration Studies*, 25, 2 (1999), 335–44.
3. For an account of another fans' group that successfully changed the direction of their club, see S. North and P. Hodson, *Build a Bonfire: How Football Fans United to Save Brighton and Hove Albion* (Edinburgh: Mainstream, 1997).
4. For an account of the life of Arthur Tull see P. Vasili, 'Walter Daniel Tull, 1888–1918: Soldier, Footballer, Black', *Race and Class*, 38, 2 (1996), 51–69. P. Vasili, *The First Black Footballer: Arthur Wharton 1865–1930* (London and Portland, OR: Frank Cass, 1998).
5. Football Task Force, *Investing in the Community* (London: Stationery Office, 1999). Football Task Force, *Football: Commercial Issues* (London: Stationery Office, 1999).
6. See chapter 3 in this volume for details of Brian Lomax's involvement in the establishment of Supporters Direct.
7. In his speech at the Labour Party conference in October 1999, Secretary of State for Culture, Media and Sport Chris Smith called for fans to become more involved in their football clubs through the setting up of trusts similar to the one described in this piece. This initiative has now taken effect with the establishment of Supporters Direct.

Notes on the Contributors

Trevor Brooking CBE was a professional footballer for West Ham United FC and England. He is now Chairman of Sport England.

Adam Brown is Research Fellow at the Institute of Popular Culture, Manchester Metropolitan University and Associate Research fellow in the Football Research Unit, Birkbeck College and was a member of the Football Task Force.

Andy Burnham is the former administrator of the Football Task Force and an Everton FC supporter.

Peter Carr is a founder member of The Celtic Trust.

Michael Crick is a writer, most notably of the best-selling biography of Lord Archer, and broadcaster. A Manchester United supporter for almost 30 years, he was one of the founders of Shareholders United Against Murdoch, and is now Vice-Chair of Shareholders United.

Peter Crowther is a consultant to Rosenblatt Solicitors and Associate Research Fellow, Birkbeck College.

Richard Faulkner was Vice Chair of the Football Task Force, 1997–99. He is a working Labour peer. From 1979 to 1998 he played a central role in the Football Trust, as trustee, secretary and latterly, deputy chairman. He was appointed as a 'public interest' non-executive director of Brighton & Hove Albion FC, at the instigation of the Football Association in 1997.

Jeanette Findlay is a founder member of The Celtic Trust, Lecturer at the Department of Urban Studies, Universty of Glasgow, and Associate Research Fellow Football Research Unit, Birkbeck College .

Sean Hamil is a founder member of The Celtic Trust, and Deputy Director, Football Research Unit, Birkbeck College .

Joe Hill is a founder member of The Celtic Trust, and National Secretary of the Scottish Co-operative Party.

Kevin Jaquiss is a solicitor with the firm of Cobbetts in Manchester. He is a legal adviser to Supporters Direct and the Co-operative movement.

Brian Lomax is Chair of Supporters Direct, was Chairman of Northampton Town FC Supporters' Trust, Director of Northampton Town FC, and is an Associate Research Fellow, Birkbeck College.

Jonathan Michie is the Sainsbury Professor of Management at Birkbeck College, a Director of Supporters Direct, and Chair of Shareholders United.

Stephen Morrow is Senior Lecturer at the Department of Sports Studies, University of Stirling.

Christine Oughton is Reader in Management and Director of the Football Research Unit, Birkbeck College .

Rt. Hon. Chris Smith MP is Secretary of State for Culture, Media and Sport, and an Arsenal FC fan.

Andy Walsh is the former Chair of the Independent Manchester United Supporters' Association.

Steven Warby is Research Officer, Birkbeck College Football Research Unit.

Trevor Watkins is Chairman, AFC Bournemouth, an Associate Research Fellow, Birkbeck College, and a Director of Supporters Direct.

Abstracts

Recent Developments in Football Ownership
Sean Hamil, Jonathan Michie, Christine Oughton and Steven Warby

Dramatic changes have occurred in the way football is organized. These include: the formation of the Premier League; the introduction of all–seater stadiums; escalating ticket prices; increasing money from TV deals; the transformation of clubs into Plcs and growing media company ownership of football clubs. Notwithstanding these changes one fact remains constant – football clubs need supporters if they are to survive and prosper. The central theme of this collection is that the positive role that supporters play in football needs to be recognized and harnessed in formal mechanisms that allow supporters a greater say in how their clubs are run. Formalizing the positive role that supporters play in football through the creation of supporters' trusts is one way of facilitating this. The government has recently launched a new policy initiative – Supporters Direct – that aims to meet this objective. Supporters Direct is a dedicated unit that provides packages of legal advice and practical assistance to groups of supporters who wish to form a trust in order to be more involved in the running of their club. The essays in this volume provide both the theoretical rationale for the formation of supporters' trusts and a series of case studies that illustrate how such trusts operate in practice.

Strengthening the Voice of Supporters
Rt. Hon. Chris Smith MP

This essay sets out the Government's rationale for the formation of Supporters Direct – a dedicated unit that provides legal and practical support for supporters to form supporters' trusts with a view to being actively involved in the way their clubs are run. The piece starts by considering two possible scenarios for the future development of football. The first scenario sees an unfettered continuation of recent trends towards greater inequality between the richest and poorest clubs and over-commercialization. The alternative scenario is to foster a competitive English league by promoting greater equality, strengthening grassroots football and encouraging closer links between football clubs and their supporters. The main argument of this study is that the second scenario requires policy initiatives that encourage all those in the game to work together – the football authorities, government and supporters. The involvement of supporters is central to this task and the Government's creation of Supporters Direct is one such initiative designed to ensure the future health of the game by giving supporters a greater say in how their clubs are run.

Episode One: May the Force Be with You!
Brian Lomax

This essay outlines the genesis and principles of the Government's new initiative – Supporters Direct – from the Football Task Force's *Investing in the Community* report published in January 1999, to the launch of Supporters Direct in August 2000. Supporters Direct is grounded in three principles: influence, ownership and representation. The piece discusses the eligibility criteria for supporters' groups to receive assistance and the work of the unit. The eligibility criteria include the need to demonstrate that the supporter groups have democratic structures that are open to all fans and representative of a broad range of supporters. Groups that meet these criteria will be eligible for a package of legal, practical and financial advice. An important part of the work of the unit is the provision of legal blueprints for the organization and operation of supporters' trusts that meet the needs of individual clubs.

United for Change
Trevor Brooking

This essay provides an assessment of the aims and objectives of Supporters Direct and shows how this initiative dovetails with the work of Sport England. It discusses the link between football clubs and their local community and the importance of strengthening these ties in order to increase interest and participation in football and sport more generally. Facilitating supporter and community involvement in football clubs is seen as an important part of this task. One of the key objectives of Sport England is to increase the numbers of people that are involved and participating in sport. The piece argues that 'football can promote social interaction and inclusion' and shows how the work of Supporters Direct complements that of Sport England in its objective to involve more people in sport.

Broadcasters v. Regulators: The Threat to Football from Media Company Ownership of Football Clubs
Peter Crowther

This study explores the grounds for intervention by the competition authorities to protect against the public interest concerns raised by media control of football clubs. The expansion of the pay-TV market has increased the amount of money flowing into football and opened up new opportunities. At the same time, it is evident that media companies have specific interests in football that may require regulatory intervention in order to ensure fair competition in broadcasting, preserve the quality of football and prevent the exploitation of consumers, in this case, football supporters. This essay outlines recent developments in media ownership of football clubs and discusses a number of possible grounds for intervention by the regulatory authorities.

The Legacy of the Football Task Force
Richard Faulkner

This piece presents the findings of the Football Task Force and provides the context in which the issue of supporter involvement in football clubs emerged onto the public agenda. The Task Force's remit is outlined and assessed and the reasons behind the presentation of differing 'minority' and 'majority' versions of the Task Force's final report and recommendations are set out. In addition to the recommendations regarding supporter involvement, an important recommendation of the majority report was the establishment of a Football Audit Commission and detailed Code of Practice to implement the report's recommendations. A central argument of this essay is that the recommendations of the majority report, including the establishment of supporters' trusts and Supporters Direct, offers the most coherent way forward for football.

Time for Change: Supporters Direct
Andy Burnham

This piece describes how the typical relationship between supporters' groups and football club owners and administrators had become characterized by distrust. It outlines how the net consequence of this legacy was negative for clubs and offers a number of examples showing how clubs have benefited by adopting a conciliatory partnership towards their supporters' organizations. The author challenges the conception commonly held by club administrators that supporters' groups lack the expertise to make a positive contribution to the effective running of their clubs. In particular, it is argued that policy initiatives such as Supporters Direct have the potential to facilitate synergy between supporters' groups and club administrators to unlock substantial benefits for both parties.

Mutualism Rules: The Community in Football
Kevin Jaquiss

This essay describes and analyses the various legal models that supporters' trusts might take. It draws on the example of the Crystal Palace Supporters' Trust and outlines the importance of the formation of the trust to supporters' efforts to save the club and seek effective supporter representation. The argument then broadens out to consider a variety of democratic, mutual and not for profit legal structures that are being developed by Supporters Direct. These include companies limited by guarantee, Industrial and Provident Societies and trusts. The piece provides analysis of the technical legal issues involved in establishing legal structures for greater supporter involvement in football clubs.

Cherries in the Black: AFC Bournmouth's Journey from Bankruptcy to Rude Health under Supporter Leadership
Trevor Watkins

This is a case study of an ordinary fan who became chairman of the club he supported. It describes how the (now) chairman and a group of colleagues led the campaign to save AFC Bournemouth from financial ruin and raised enough money to buy the club with the help of a Community Trust. The discussion gives detailed analysis of the pitfalls and skills necessary for any group of supporters contemplating an active role in club management. The analysis makes a powerful case for the concept of trusts as a means of saving clubs facing bankruptcy and as a way of encouraging greater supporter involvement on the board.

Shareholders United Against Murdoch
Michael Crick

It is not just the supporters of small, lower league clubs who are seeking greater representation and involvement in football. This piece provides a detailed case study of the activities of shareholding Manchester United supporters and the formation of Shareholders United. It describes how Shareholders United evolved from a group of supporters who came together to campaign against the proposed takeover of Manchester United by BSkyB into a fully fledged supporter-shareholder organization seeking wider share ownership among supporters and representation of this group's interests to the club. The piece assesses the successes and difficulties of establishing working relations with a club. The central conclusion is that organizations such as Shareholders United have a vital role to play as part of the checks and balances needed in an era of increasing commercialization in football.

The Celtic Trust
Peter Carr, Sean Hamil, Joe Hill, Jeanette Findlay and Stephen Morrow

This essay outlines the genesis of the organization of The Celtic Trust at Celtic Football Club. It shows how several aspects of the club's historical development have facilitated the formation of The Celtic Trust. These include the social roots of the club as a charitable self-help organization and the decision of Fergus McCann, the former owner of a controlling interest in Celtic, to sell his shares to existing supporter-shareholders and season-ticket holders. This decision has created a window of opportunity for supporters who wish to exercise more influence over how the club is administered. The authors assess the progress of the Trust, the obstacles overcome, and conclude by presenting a detailed outline of the Celtic Trust 'Statement of Principles' document on which the formal constitution of the organization – which was registered as an Industrial and Provident Society in September 2000 – was based.

Football Supporters' Relations with Their Clubs: A European Perspective
Adam Brown and Andy Walsh

The authors consider supporter involvement in football clubs in a European context by charting the extent of fan representation and participation in Italy, Spain and Germany. They analyse supporter involvement in these countries in the differing overall context of: the historical role of supporters' organizations; how different European football clubs are organized and run; and the differing issues of access. The essay describes the activities of the *ultras* in Italy, club membership organizations such as L'Elefant Blau in Spain, and supporters' reactions to the more cautious approach to commercialism taken by football clubs in Germany. Although it is difficult to draw direct comparisons, the authors suggest that pressures on the game similar to those in the UK – the effects of the *Bosman* ruling, increases in expenditure, the role of media companies and so on – may produce greater politicization of supporter organizations across the Continent.

How Democracy Saved Northampton Town FC
Brian Lomax

Lomax recounts the history of Northampton Town Supporters' Trust, the first such trust to be formed in British football. He attempts to analyse the impact the trust has made upon the life of the Football Club, which was also the first to admit elected supporters' representatives to full Directorships. The benefits have been not only financial, but also social – leading to closer links between the football club and the local authority and fostering community development. The essay concludes by listing the necessary conditions for supporters' democracy and representation to be effective in football clubs generally.

Index